Discover
A Personal Journey through the Lives and Works of James and Betty Durden

*For the Durden-Hey family
and for the Roberts Family,
and Aneirin and Anwen Woodward*

Ros Roberts

BOOKCASE

Poppies by James Durden

Contents

Prologue	5
1: A Cycle Ride	8
2: Student Days	11
3: Tramping Fleet Street	15
4: Moving On	23
5: Ruby	30
6: Darling Heart	37
7: Two Paintings in the Summer of 1915	55
8: Private Durden	63
9: Millbeck	69
10: Betty	85
11: The Bridesmaid	104
12: Fame	108
13: Portraits and People	125
14: Shipwreck	144
15: The Webster Portrait Mystery	150
16: A Sense of Place	153
17: Rabbit Holes!	172
18: Rest in Peace	184

James Durden and Betty

Prologue

It all started with . . .

An E-MAIL dated 22nd of September, 2020 From: Ros Roberts, a Research Volunteer at Keswick Museum and Art Gallery To: Janet Durden-Hey, living on the Isle of Skye, the grand-daughter of the artist James Durden.

An article appeared in the Cumberland News September 13th,1952, announcing an EXHIBITION of OIL and WATER COLOUR PAINTINGS By JAMES. DURDEN, R.O.I.

And a bequest to Keswick Museum of *eight pictures from Mr J. Durden of Millbeck Place, Millbeck on permanent loan.* Durden gave the paintings to the Museum in memory of his wife Ruby Valentina Ellis, who died on April 21st 1958. This became a confirmed bequest in December 2011 by the Durden-Hey Family.

And that e-mail: *We are hoping to run a mini exhibition in part of the refurbished building on the beautiful and important paintings executed by your grandfather. This is planned for March of next year . . . At the moment I am attempting to put together material for some information panels to accompany the display of paintings. We hope to focus on: Our paintings on display; The magazine and book illustrations; The context of the 1920's (music, fashion etc); The artistic style; A biography of James.*

I wonder if you would be able to help with any details of the latter. A photograph and permission to use it would be lovely if you felt able to provide such an artefact (and any other appropriate materials).

I live in Applethwaite near Keswick so am quite close to the

5

lovely house where your grandparents lived and have a copy of 'Summer in Cumberland' from Manchester Art Gallery on my living room wall. It is just about my favourite painting and cheers me up through the sometimes grey winters round here when the fells disappear from view! I'm sure you will understand that living in Skye, rather grander than the Lake District but also prone to some spectacular winter conditions!
Thank you for your kind attention on this matter. My details are below.

Sincerely,
Ros Roberts

Much to to my delight, this unsolicited letter met with a kind and interested response from Janet Durden-Hey, She was indeed the daughter of Joseph, who was Durden's only son. Her father had died as had her aunt Betty, but Janet had inherited various documents relating to her grandfather.

Janet sent me a usb stick. I can still remember my exhilaration at opening this file and finding James Durden staring back at me. It was the photograph of him in his First World War army uniform. He looked so handsome, but there was the slightest jaunty tip to the regulation hat and definitely a twinkle in his eye. Suddenly the possible exhibition of his spectacular paintings became more of a reality. I was hooked by the man as well as the artist.

The following May Janet and her husband David Hey kindly made the trip from Skye to Keswick. She walked into my kitchen that cloudy Spring evening clutching a blue plastic box which she deposited on the kitchen table. In it was what she knew of her grandfather's life. Such treasure in a plastic box … letters, his sketch book, carefully torn out sections of magazines, proof copies of book illustrations, photographs, a scrap book, newspaper reviews and random details of sales of the Millbeck house and various paintings. A wedding certificate and a death certificate but no birth certificate or any details of his war service.

I took Janet and David up to the Durden house, Millbeck Place which Janet hadn't seen since the time she spent there with her grandfather, at the age of 16 and then visited Crosthwaite

Churchyard where I had found his grave. Janet had also brought with her a beautiful portfolio of Betty's paintings. Plainly Betty had inherited her father's artistic gene and the book showed her flair for print design and repeating patterns in exquisite watercolour paintings. Betty was also Durden's principal model until her marriage to Leonard Green, an Australian, took her away from England. In the event the Museum was able to focus the Exhibition on Betty as well as James.

    With impressive magnanimity Janet agreed to lend us this family archive and I concentrated on writing the information panels and an information booklet for the Exhibition. We managed to locate some of the paintings still in the local area and borrowed them to join the ones which came up from the Art store. The Durden-Hey family lent us some beautiful, hitherto unseen paintings. The exhibition went ahead with suitable period razzmatazz of context in the 1930s and we all learned to do the Charleston! It was fun and certainly brought James' prodigious talent to the notice of the general public with so much hitherto unknown and unseen material. We now had access to delightful bird, animal, flora and fauna paintings done when this Manchester lad was only 16 and then as a scholarship student, at the Royal College of Art. These all went on display in glass cases. Certificates and Awards, personal photographs of the family (including Chu the dog) in the caravan in Cornwall, all drew interest and discussion

    However, so much was left unsaid and unrecognized and I gained Janet's permission to pursue some further research and embark on a book about this talented artist and kind unassuming gentleman. I have held true to the knowledge that this is a local man who belongs in this village as well as the wider Art world. I know he has enjoyed and engaged with all this quiet and peaceful place has to offer and I can see why he made it his artistic home. His understanding of how the changing light, colour, reflection and landscape works in the Lake District will be preserved forever in his paintings..

    This is a 'Spots of Time' story for James Durden, artist and gentleman.

1: A Cycle Ride

The Summer of 1895 was a cracking one. The sun rose in a blaze of pink light every day, illuminating the fells and shimmering over the high tarns. Everything rejoiced from skylarks to farmers and the world seemed briefly to be a better place.

Approaching the shores of Lake Windermere comes a young man on a borrowed bicycle. The bike is a heavy machine with solid tyres and the young chap is struggling a little to balance his flapping jacket and canvas rucksack and keep the recalcitrant machine under control on the lengthy hundred mile trek from Manchester to Cumberland. Now within sight of Windermere his driving motivation is paying off: he is bewitched. He dismounts.

The view - the serenity of the lake and the range of steepling fells - is spectacular and he is lost for words. He is seeing exactly what he came to see. His artistic eye sees the lines of colour, structure, tone and light, (yes especially that special light), and speaks volumes to him. The weariness of the bike ride is forgotten. He knows with heartfelt intuition that this is a land for an artist. This is where he is meant to be. The grime and poverty of his industrial Manchester home fade. He lets the reality of his surroundings take over the images only previously seen in books and created in his imagination.

His name is James …. James Durden and he has made this mammoth lone trip to see for himself the glories talked of by other students and friends at the Art college in Manchester. He is 17 and is already showing evidence of a prodigious talent. Some beautiful watercolours of birds produced the previous year have come to the notice of others and been highly acclaimed.

Gathering his scattered thoughts James remounts his bike

eager now to continue his journey. He is heading for a little village outside Keswick called Ormathwaite. He has lodgings with Isabella and John Richardson of Birkett Farm. At Grasmere James pauses again to examine the little white Dove Cottage.

He approaches Dunmail Raise and realises the only way he will make any progress is to push the dratted bike up an impressive looking incline. The freewheel down to Wythburn Water is an exhilarating descent with magnificent views of the two lakes and the three little bridges separating Wythburn Water from Leathes Water. With mounting excitement, our artist is soon approaching the little market town of Keswick. He marvels at the magnificent amphitheatre of the Derwent fells and the gleam of the lake below him. He is thrilled with this new environment and completely enchanted by the brilliant clear light showing every path and tree in form and structure on the fells. It's such a new world and he is captivated.

Keswick is busy . . . it is market day and James pushes the bike through the broad market square passing loaded carts positioned on the cobbles round a rather quirky building known as the Moot Hall. He buys a chunk of cheese and some bread and rather reluctantly abandons the town and heads out to find Applethwaite.

With the market behind him, the road out of the town quietens dramatically and the view is now dominated by the massive bulk of Skiddaw. The midday sun highlights the fell. As he skirts round the edge of Latrigg James promises himself he will climb this mountain soon. He pedals the last few 100 yards up the Ormathwaite road towards Applethwaite and stops the bike again to look for the old waterwheel at the edge of the farm. As he turns right, over the beck and follows the bend in the track the farmhouse comes into view nestling in the little thicket of trees. It is a solid four square building with a whitewashed frontage, a rather worn gable end and a porch that faces not out front as expected but away from the path and up towards the woods on Latrigg.

Even at first glance James can see that it must have been constructed like that to escape the prevailing wind. Attached is a solid looking long barn which is used for livestock, fodder storage and machinery.

Isabella Richardson is outside the porch. She dries her hands on her ample apron before welcoming her holiday lodger. John doesn't like strangers in the house, but sees the sense in taking in paying visitors. He quite takes to this young chap eager to know everything about the farm and the country-side. He stoically answers the constant questions covering everything from the sort of sheep on Latrigg to the doings of Keswick and its occupants.

So James Durden, the young art student, arrives in the Lake District for the first time in that summer of 1895. His first walk from the cottage probably took him up the track from the porch, through the woods onto the fell and up to the summit of Latrigg. There he would be able to see the whole of Keswick nestled in the valley beneath him and the mighty encampment of fells stretching above the lake to the Borrowdale valley and beyond. Maybe he descended down the front track into the town and perhaps wandered along the river in the park to see where Robert Southey used to live. He may have come across the new firebrand preacher who was causing so much a stir in Keswick, one Canon Rawnsley. He almost certainly walked or cycled and along the terrace road passed the Sunday School Room and along to Millbeck to see the old woollen Mill now sadly redundant. He must have climbed Skiddaw. And he had a bicycle, so did he venture further afield? Perhaps to Bassenthwaite and up the Borrowdale valley.

Whatever Durden did, the Lake District made a deep and lasting impression on his young artistic heart, mind and soul. He returned home to Manches-ter to be granted a scholarship to the Royal College of Art in London.

10

2: Student Days

James Durden was born on November 29th, 1877 to James and Mary Ellen (nee Swarbrick) at 17 March Street, Manchester. His father was 'a maker up of cotton goods'

Two other events occurred in 1877 which significantly influenced James' path through life. The first was the birth of another boy on the 13th November. His father was Robert Walter Wraithman Webster, a 'salesman'. His mother Mary was the daughter of a bookkeeper, Edwin Lowe. He was baptised Walter Ernest in Manchester Cathedral on the 10th January,1878. He grew up to be a prestigious figure and portrait painter and illustrator. These two boys became lifelong friends, moving in similar artistic circles and following the same career paths.

That same year, land was purchased at Cavendish Street for a new building for the Manchester School of Art in Mosely Street. George Tunstall Redmayne was appointed architect and designed the ashlar sandstone building with terracotta dressing. It was an impressive structure with a symmetrical facade built in Neo Gothic style with large gabled wings and a chamfered doorway.

I have been unable to locate any detail about Durden's early education in Manchester, but his daughter, Betty, stares that he attended the Manchester School of Art. However, he was awarded a Scholarship to the Royal College of Art when he was 17.

There is evidence of Durden's early talent in some pencil sketches and beautiful watercolours of native birds. A sketch from 1894, of a 'Major Tit' shows a bird gleaning insects off its perch on a thin branch. The pecking movements of this long tailed tit are beautifully suggested. Another watercolour on card shows a bullfinch, with its black head, balanced on a branch and focused on something below its eyes. The accuracy of the red coloured breast and the shading of extended wings and darker tail capture the appearance of the bird, which he labels, 'Pyrrhula Pyrrhula… Bullfinch...Britain . . . nearly lifesize'. Two further bird studies, a Tree Sparrow and a Brambling, are alive and accurate and are highly impressive for such early student paintings.

Further undated drawings and paintings of flowers and animals, possibly college exercises, were made around about this time, One, an open Lily shows the petals against a rather unexpectedly solid black background, making a flamboyant statement about delicate petals and stamens. The impression is one of strength rather than fragility.

A foolscap sheet, dated 1895, was executed in London and shows three excellent pencil sketches of a greyhound or whippet. A more complete pencil sketch of a long haired Welsh collie shows the left back leg slightly ahead of the right giving the impression that the dog is in mid-movement. The proportions are perfect and details of the long haired coat, the curve of the upright tail and the set of the ruff and head with ears pricked up make a really delightful sketch. The Royal College of Art must have been the perfect environment for Durden as a young Art student and it gave him every opportunity to develop his talent and learn the finer skills of his craft.

The next portfolio of sketches in the archive has a page dated May 17th /97 with the location as Hyde Park. It shows a small pencil sketch of a tree trunk with impressive shading revealing every nuance of the ancient gnarled trunk, complete with fissures, breaks and ancient knotholes. Further pages in this folder include a small sheet with two bird wings done in ink with every feather's detail showing and a larger pencil study of a Great Black-backed gull. There's a preliminary sketch of drapery and two larger bold pencil sketches of how material would fall from a costume. Durden is learning the skills later exemplified in his paintings of Betty in her exquisite flowing dresses against the backdrops of fine draperies and differing textiles.

    A set of sepia photographs shows how Durden thrived at the College. One shows twelve young men and three ladies sitting in the open air together on a high backed bench. The men wear suits and straw boaters. Durden is seated casually on one arm of the bench. The three ladies are wearing highnecked blouses in the Victorian style. Two of the ladies carry parasols . It is a posed picture and the students are not smiling. However they do look very relaxed and at ease with themselves. In another, every-one's pose has slipped and two chaps on the back row are making a fist to fist loop of some sort. Both have pipes or cigarettes and, judging by the profile, one of them is Durden.

    In another, the ladies have disappeared and a larger group of eighteen jolly gentlemen are caught in a rather different pose. The front row of twelve men form a merry dancing troupe with each one gripping the shoulders of the chap in front and all swinging one leg in a parallel movement to the right. The suits are still there, but looking considerably more creased and dishevelled and every-one is smiling or laughing. James is a distinc-tive figure on the front row wearing his northern flat cap in a rather stylish way with his pipe clenched firmly between his teeth.

College Days

The students modelled for each other and several pictures show James dressed up in different costumes from a mediaeval look to what appears to be a Hussar. Four small photos show an interior studio /art room at the College with students scattered about and working on what looks like a copying exercise. One picture catches these young men relaxing around it in mid conversation. Durden is the only one standing and he is leaning casually against a bicycle parked in quite a random fashion behind him.

The ladies appear rarely, but one photograph from 1899 shows all James' contemporary group. It's a happy sunny afternoon where everyone is smiling or laughing. James is semi-reclining on the rough grass on the front row of three. In this little trio his opposite number has adopted the same pose and both men are carrying tennis racquets. James is holding his racquet as if he is strumming a guitar . He wears a frivolous grin.

I have studied the faces of the young ladies very carefully in the hope of seeing Ruby Ellis (James' future wife) as part of this group. It's not known exactly where James and Ruby met. Janet thinks that Ruby possibly went to the Slade School of Fine Art and they well have met up during those Art College days. The student photographs extend to 1899. James and Ruby must have been together round about this period as 4 photographs show James with the Ellis family in 1900 ….. with James looking a little uncomfortable and rather out of his comfort zone.

Whatever his social situation James studied assiduously. Two certificates record evidence of considerable achievement in different disciplines. At the 'Examination in Drawing from the Life', Subject 8c2 held on the 30th April 1898, 1,350 candidates presented themselves. James Durden obtained a First Class in the above-named subject. *At the 'Examination in Modelling, Design', James was one of 269 awarded a First Class out of a total entry of 627. He also obtained First Class Honours in Design..*

3: Tramping Fleet Street

James Durden stayed in London as it offered better career prospects and opportunities. The 1901 census records James, 23, a 'self (employed) artist-painter', as an occupant of 71, Chelverton Road, Putney. The head of the household is Mary Webster, aged 45 and her family members are listed as daughter, Gertrude aged 25, 'a governess' and son, Walter E, 23, James's friend, who was another 'self artist (painter)' There were three other lodgers, Harold Breach, 29, a repairman; Herbert Lawrence, a 22 year old architect; and Thomas C Drysdale, a 20 year old art student. Significantly, all the occupants on this census were born in or near Manchester. James is in Chelverton Road in 1901, but moved to an address in Jubilee Road by the time Ruby was writing to him in January 1902.

He started "tramping Fleet Street" to look for work in his last year at the Royal College of Art.. Once they left Art College it looks as if Durden and Webster may have rented and shared a studio together and certainly both attempted initially to break into the ephemeral genre of illustrations for magazines.

Durden, who was good at coming up with ideas to illustrate stories, probably gained a reputation for reliability and meeting deadlines. As his reputation grew he was able to get work with book publishers as well. At some point he acquired an agent. Rather unusually this was a woman, Miss Enid Balchin who lived at 154, Dora Road, Wimbledon Park, London.

In this section of the Archive there is an extensive collection of loose torn-out pages and also a brown sketch book. The pages have been collected together with no concern given to the dates.

There are several pages torn from the Strand Magazine,

Volume 50, 1915). Pages 565 to 572 feature an extract from a story called 'The Pavilion' by Edith Nesbit, illustrated by James Durden. The pictures show the two main characters Ernestine and Amelia in full crinoline dresses 'with muslin flounces' and two young gentlemen, one of whom comes to a fatal end in the Pavilion. Durden has treated the readers to a magnificent double page illustration for the caption: *"She sat there in the white ring of her crinoline dress like a broken white rose. But her arms were round Thesiger and she would not move them"*.

In 'The Adventure' in the 'Lady's Realm' magazine Durden has given full range to his talents to portray the tragic dying moments of heroine Ellen: *"She made a wonderful picture, Sister Mary thought, as she lay gazing up at the sky in awed delight, her lips parted by a rapt smile of content, the white lilies lying on her breast, her loose auburn hair transformed by the sunbeams into a living halo of gold"*. The magazine was issued after the Battle of the Marne, 5th-12th September 1914. There is a piece of finger-posted advice at the top of this page: *"If you have no friend in the Army or Navy to whom you can send this magazine, you may hand it in at any post office, without any address or wrapper, and it will be forwarded free of charge to some ship, trench, or hospital where it will be appreciated"*.

Another single page of *The Lady's Realm* has written on it in pencil *'Durden and Webster'* so the two artists were still collaborating on the bread and butter work. Durden's reputation grew and magazines were more prepared to acknowledge his contributions. Doctor Rabanus has the byline 'Written for Albert Kinross. Illustrated by J.Durden'. I'm not sure who collected all the Durden cuttings in the Archive. It could have been his agent, Enid Balchin, or Ruby. Whatever their origin it's a delight to see that such ephemera has survived well over a hundred years.

One picture carries the words *"Agatha in her troubles consults the most famous fortune teller in London"*. This portrays a rather mysterious young female figure in Arabian type head cover, standing over some sort of flaming structure. An orb of fire hovers way above the flames and the fortune teller appears to be interpreting swirling pictures within this fiery ball.

Durden obviously worked extremely hard during these years. His illustrations are all detailed and beautifully executed drawings or paintings. There is no indication that they were hasty or rough: the magazines expected a high standard of skill.

One file of 27 torn out pictures gives a random selection of his work, including some book as well as magazine illustrations. A faint editorial stamp on a picture showing a lady and gentleman in a garden with a delightful thatched cottage in the background, reads 'Rough proof for size'.

All extracts now show the familiar signature, simply DURDEN quite often (but not always) in a box with a scroll effect. These illustrations show the unmistakable artistic style which Durden would go on to develop in his portraits of Betty and others, especially with the interior backgrounds and costumes. One picture shows two gentlemen seated in wing armchairs with a decorative free standing folding screen behind. The screen has a peacock motif with detailed long tails draped down the pattern surrounded by blossoms. It's very similar to the background used in the Betty and Chou picture of later years.

Another picture again features crinolines and top hats with a lady standing by door in a side street and about to unlock it. A young gentleman in attendance is declaring: *I must see you again . . . It is absolutely necessary. When can I see you and where?*

A further cutting illustrates a play script as opposed to a story. It's difficult to tell if this too featured in a magazine or as a stand alone complete script. It appears to portray a love story featuring the French aristocracy, but again the print is compromised by the enthusiastic scissors of the collector. The illustration shows a highly fashionable young lady and two gentlemen with a footman bowing in the forefront of the picture and obviously presenting a small item for inspection .The caption reads *You prefer the pearl in a golden setting? A pretty wit, Monsieur!*

The illustration demonstrates the characteristic accuracy and

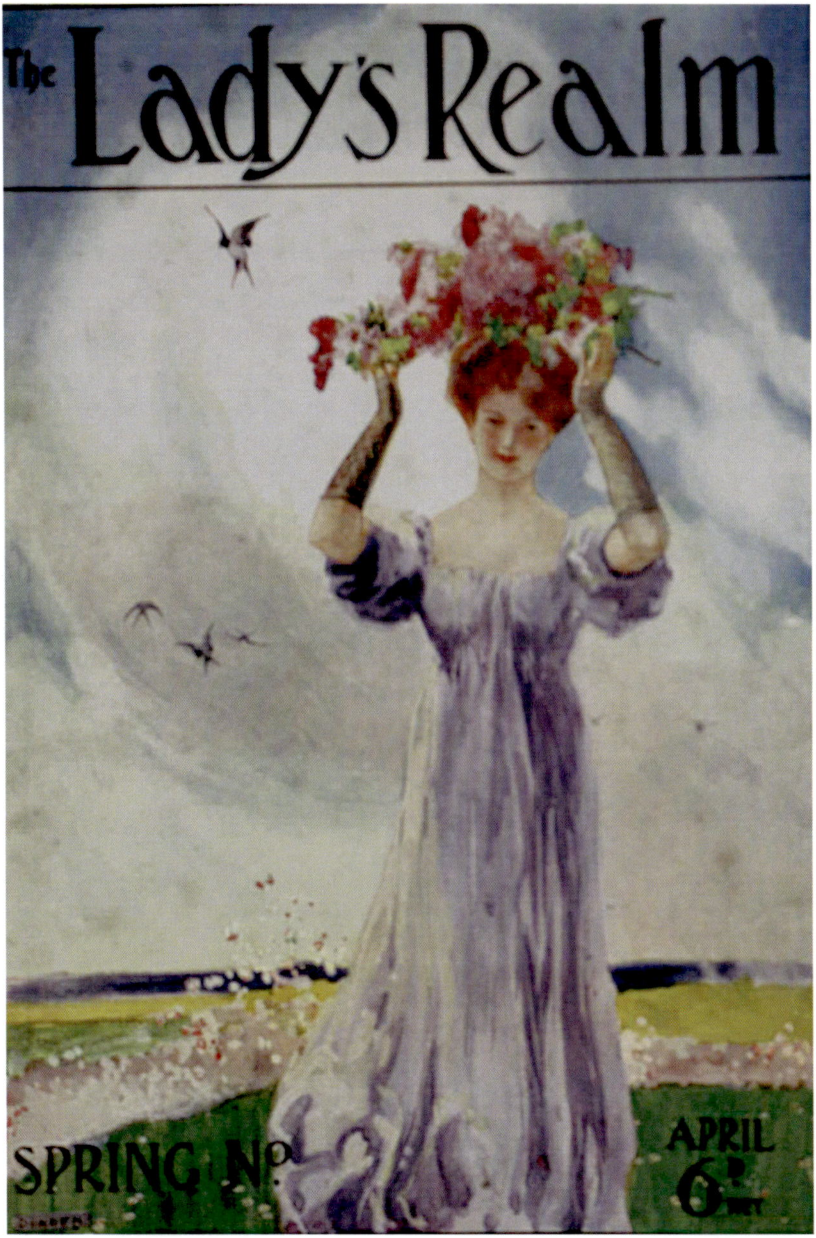
The Lady's Realm
SPRING No.
APRIL
6

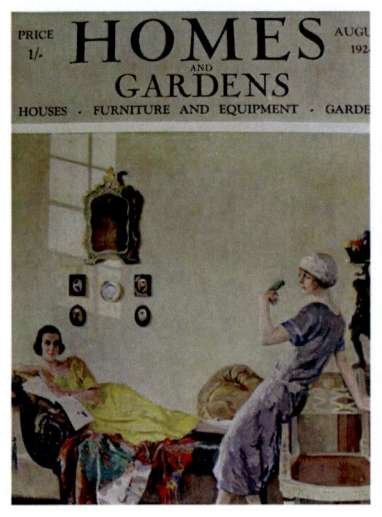

detail of a Durden picture, but the usual small signature in the corner is slightly different. He usually signs in capital letters just the surname in a box, sometimes with scroll surround. However on this occasion he has used his full name JAMES DURDEN and miraculously the date ... 1901. This indicates a transition time from the Royal College of Art and also highlights early success. The signature must have been refined as he progressed.

Durden illustrations started to appear on the front covers of some prestigious magazines. A Spring edition of the *Lady's Realm* dated April (but no year) and priced 6d has a full length figure of an attractive young lady wearing a flowing low cut lilac gown. The folds of delicate fabric are presented in true Durden style. Accessories consist of elbow length black lacy gloves and a spectacular hat. This hat is a cornucopia of tumbling Spring flowers in bright and pale pink blossoms and lilac flowers. The multicoloured sky of greys, lilacs and pastel swirling clouds gives way to hopeful strand of bright blue. Staying true to his ornithological abilities, Durden has painted some swallows heralding Spring and they are delightfully accurate ... a lovely addition to this Spring sky. It's a beautiful front cover to the magazine.

As Durden moved into the realms of serious painting, there was no longer any need to illustrate for magazines as his paintings themselves were in demand for use as front covers. The cover for the November Homes and Gardens Magazine in 1925 shows a sitting room lit by a table lamp and firelight and creates an ambience of warmth, comfort and cosiness. A small soft sofa covered in pale yellow flowered chintz holds three sagging, obviously comfortable cushions, a throw and an open book with a page standing up where the reader has just left it. An occasional circular table is on hand containing the tray with a silver tea pot and coffee pot. Another half moon table to the right of the sofa contains the lamp, more books and a small bowl of bronze white and yellow chrysanthemums. This tranquil picture is completed by the black and white cat snoozing on the red rug in front of the fire.

In very small print at the bottom of the magazine cover it says *By the Fireside* from the painting by James Durden. This room is recognisably the sitting room at Millbeck Place. Ruby Durden completed the purchase of this delightful Georgian house in Millbeck in 1924 and the family were well settled by 1925. 'Summer in Cumberland' was painted there in 1925 and various features of the room and family life show up in both pictures. The most obvious and appealing detail is the family cat, whose distinctive black and white markings reveal him to be the same cat as the one at Ruby's feet in the summer sunshine of the afternoon tea. The silver tray is the same one as is the teapot and coffee pot and even the same green tea service stands up to closer scrutiny. With this magazine cover we now have representations of Summer and Winter in Millbeck Place. Both pictures capture the ambience of the respective seasons with the delights of the bright summer sunshine showing up in stark contrast to the comfort and cosiness of the darker winter months.

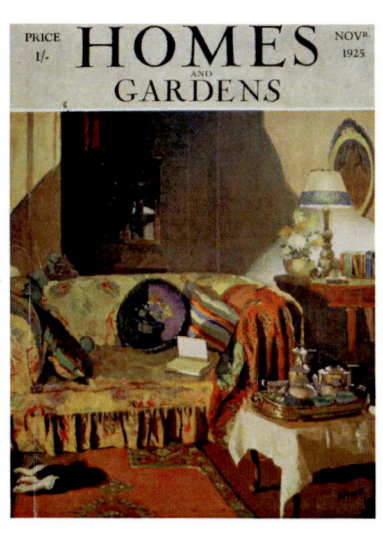

Durden's magazine work also appears on covers of foreign magazines. One issue of the Danish 'Tidens Kvinder', (Women Of the Time) shows the familiar Betty and Chu picture with its turquoise background and another one is simply called Betty, but is the original Bridesmaid painting. Details on the front covers give the titles and artist. They may be as late as 1955.

The final gem in the Archive is a brown Sketch Book manufactured by George Rowney and Co. It contains 30 leaves and the collector has filled up 28 of the pages with book proof pictures and magazine cuttings. These may have been collected and mounted by Ruby Durden. Unlike the loose pages she has now has taken the pains to cut out magazine pages and glue them carefully into this scrap book. Inside the front cover of the book is a small cream printed card with Mr James Durden in italic printing and hand printed underneath in black ink is the aforementioned agent Miss Enid Balchin of Dora Road, Wimbledon Park

There is evidence in here of commissions. Durden illustrated an advertisement for a P and O Cruise, drawing the bow of a spectacular cruise ship. The viewpoint gives a low perspective of this enor-mous ship rising above the waves. The wording informs readers *A Pleasure Cruise to Norway and Denmark can be under-taken on a 16 day voyage.* Another advertisement is for a Pleasure Cruise to Norway and Denmark. The illustration features a Norwegian fjord with precipitous cliffs and rocky summits surrounding an approaching ship. Glaciers and snow complete the dramatic seascape and the steepling horizon is reflected in the water below.

Another striking magazine page shows a nurse in a World War 1 uniform standing by an empty hospital bed. She is holding a a telegram and the torn opened envelope rests on the bedside table next to a bowl of roses. In the background an open window shows three soldiers, one of whom has a bandaged head. The other two are in conversation with another nurse. The tragedy of the illustration rests with the beautiful young nurse lost in thought and obvious distress.

The archive of Durden's illustration work also contained an extensive collection of pages either torn from actual fiction works or reproduced possibly as proof copies and forwarded to Durden for approval. Again they were carefully collected but with frustratingly little detail. Whatever the provenance they provide evidence of Durden's progress within the publishing houses of the day. Durden was moving on!

4: Moving On

With the early years of the new century, Durden left his student days behind and moved on to freelance work in Fleet Street. Most significantly his relationship with a young lady called Ruby Valentina Ellis developed and moved on to a serious level. Ruby was the daughter of a wealthy self-made man, Joseph Ellis and his wife, Sarah Martha Ellis. Joseph, the son of a poor handloom weaver in Saddleworth, had worked his way up to becoming a magnate of the iron and steel industry in West Cumberland. It's not known exactly where James and Ruby met but it's likely that their paths crossed in the student art world, possibly in Manchester and certainly in London. I will introduce Ruby properly in the next chapter. She was out of the country for some periods of time between 1901 and 1902, but her letters to James at this time survived and they provide fascinating evidence of her side of the romance.

As James Durden's reputation grew, he was able to gain entry into the book publishing world. He was producing illustrations for such prestigious companies as Hodder and Stoughton, Cassells, Macdonald and Evans and Henry Frowde.

This was the Golden Age of Book Illustration. There was a strong market for high quality illustrated books, which were popular as Christmas gifts. These beautifully bound deluxe editions were often followed by smaller quarto trade editions and later more modestly presented octavo editions of the more popular stories. This was the world of artists as diverse as Arthur Rackham, 1867-1939 and Mabel Lucie Attwell 1879-1964.

One of the books illustrated by Durden was *The Five Macleods* by Christina Gowan Whyte, written in 1908. Durden provided a frontispiece for the adventures undertaken by these five spirited young ladies. Elspeth, Winifred, Lil, Dorothy and Barbara become involved in all manner of escapades quite often wearing high necked broderie anglaise blouses with navy blue bows adorning the three plait hairstyle! Much of the story takes place around Lochmyle described as *a green hill - encircled loch lying cosily in the shelter of high mountains beyond, mountains separated by valleys of further lochs, so that they gained the beautiful grey blue tones of distance, and a manner of climbing into the skies and occasionally disappearing in the clouds there, which rather reminded one of the grand aloofness of some of the Lochmyle people themselves.* There was plenty of scope here for Durden to produce the beautiful frontispiece showing several boats on the loch. Miss Madeleine Delaforce, from the neighbouring country house, stands on the jetty intent on handing over a picnic basket of biscuits (rather surprisingly described as 'cookies'). Closer inspection of this picture reveals the names on the two flat bottomed rowing boats just moored in the foreground of the picture and only partially shown. Delightfully they are called Betty and Ruby!

James Durden's work is usually acknowledged with his name appearing either on the frontispiece (*With illustrations in colour by James Durden*) or with his usual signature (surname in capital letters) on the illustration.

Most of the archive consists of loose pages and these may well have been proof copies forwarded to James for inspection before final publication. Some are postcard sized whilst others are the traditional book size of illustrations (5" x 7½")

24

The Brown Sketch Book referred to in the previous chapter has a range of further Post-card sized copies of book illustrations mounted with three to a page. The range of material is extensive and covers both adult and children's books. Frustratingly, there are no labels, dates or captions.

Within these press cuttings we can see the emphasis on the genre of boys' adventure with examples of high drama, catastrophes, derring-do, rescues on both land and sea and near-death situations. One shows a boy being swept down a river in a ravine. The painting highlights the movement of the fast flowing current as it sweeps passed the precipitous cliff faces. The boy is partly submerged, but his face is still above the water so perhaps all is not lost! In another picture a small boy sits on a garden seat and the viewer is given a vision of his thoughts in the ghostly figures floating above his young head. To a lesser extent girls too are involved in crisis situations. One picture shows a young girl who has obviously slipped off a cliff path and is now hanging precariously from a single branch of a sapling above a fearful drop below. Her hat has fallen from her braided hair, but must have been secured by elastic or ribbon as it rests neatly on her shoulder. The white dress is accentuated by the scarlet ribbons at the end of her plaits.

One publishing firm, Henry Frowde and Hodder and Stoughton, did attempt to cover the interests of both sexes by publishing Herbert Strang's Library. An advert states *the library is illustrated with colour plates, reproduced by three-colour process from designs by H. M. Brock, James Durden, A Webb and other well known artists; and is issued in the following editions:-*
1. With a picture cover and coloured frontispiece, at 6d. net
2. In decorated cloth boards, with two colour plates,at 1/-.
3.In elegant cloth binding with full gilt binding and back, and four coloured plates at 2/- .
4. In handsome cloth with a picture panel on the cover, gilt edges, and four coloured plates at 2/6d.

By the time Ethne St Ives began her school adventures in *The Unwilling School Girl* published in 1913, Durden was established as a well known illustrator. There is considerable scope for his artistic talents illustrations for some of the listed books. One picture of *The Judgement of Portia* depicts her in full crimson lawyer's robes addressing the court with the stereo-typical presentation of Shylock the Jew in black cultural costume and holding the knife that he intended using to take the pound of Antonio's flesh. The latter is in the background showing a rather smug expression, presumably meant to convey his relief. It's a striking portrayal and Durden has accurately captured the drama of the moment. An equally excellent picture accompanies the moment in *As You Like It* when Rosalind as Ganymede *finds papers in the trees* in the forest of Arden. It's the height of summer and the old gnarled tree behind Rosalind is in full bloom with suitable attractive foliage around her. Touchstone, still in Elizabethan court traditional jester costume, sits at her feet and Jaques leans over a low branch to listen to her declaiming poetic tributes from Orlando. It's a good moment to illustrate with the full use of dramatic irony for the reader of the book, as presented in story form by Charles and Mary Lamb.

Illustrations for historical fiction include a resplendent Queen Elizabeth on her throne surrounded by several courtiers. She appears to be granting an audience to a figure simply clad in a long brown robe. The caption reads *Campion before Queen Elizabeth.* Two illustrations reflect the imperialism of the time. One shows a low sandy beach where a defenceless white man is being attacked by a fearful looking native in a grass skirt wielding a long knife. Another similar picture shows three white men pushing a boat out to sea. A dozen or so natives stream down the beach in angry and aggressive mood brandishing spears. The backdrop of pale yellow sand and palm trees which merge together in a haze of green and yellow produce a vivid and dramatic picture.

Although not identified, the small postcard size collection does give one clue as to origin. On the back of the Elizabethan judgement vote picture *Not Guilty,* there is a faint pencil note.

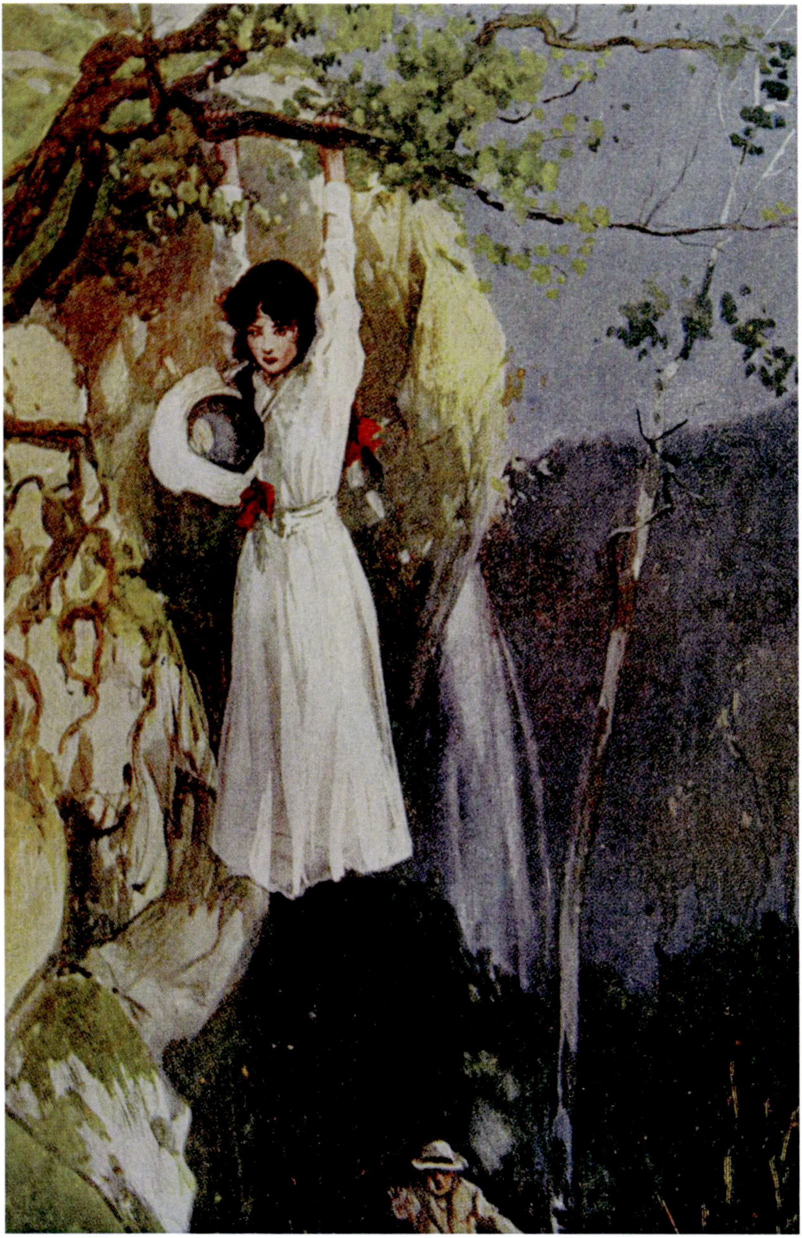

This reads *Jas Durden, Redcot, Claygate, Surrey* with the words *Reproduction, No.12, Publisher MacDonald and Evans, Adam Street, Adelphi.* Three further examples numbered 9,10 and 11 also have the publisher's name on the back - Henry Frowde and Hodder and Stoughton with the words *joint com-mittee*. Some also have the remains of brown mounts on the back looking very much as if they have been extracted from the Brown Sketch Book, which does have several empty pages in the middle.

The Brown Scrap book also contains a collection of black and white reproductions towards the back. They are differing sizes and it's impossible to establish whether they are book or magazine illustrations. The size is the only guideline as obviously the larger examples have been torn out of magazines, but some may be for books. They are all of the popular fiction genre with ladies in various anxious poses and gentlemen either playing the hero, the villain or the confidante. One features a horse drawn sleigh moving at speed through snow covered mountains and forest. Lilian (presumably the heroine) is admonishing the gentlemen *'to drive more carefully'*. Social occasions also proliferate and the Durden style is seen emerging, with dramatic backdrops featuring draped curtains, vases of flowers as accessories and ladies dressed in beautiful flowing gowns.

The Sketch Book also has one stunning original watercolour. It is oval-shaped, and marks on the back indicate that it may have been mounted in the sketch book at some point. Fortunately it is loose, as the back also has a detailed pencil sketch of a back view of a lady in an evening gown. The stance and faint hint of a circular stool implies that she is seated and would suggest that she is playing a piano. It's almost as if Durden had picked up the first piece of card that came to hand to rough out this sketch. The real painting on the front is a watercolour of a lady with a parasol which she is holding down at an angle from her body. She is also holding the front of her elegant Edwardian gown clear of the ground beneath her feet. Its double frill of orange/red polka dot fabric is highlighted by a spray of matching roses, presumably growing by the path. The broad brimmed hat shades her face and her slightly turned head suggests she may be responding to a situation in the distance . . . maybe someone has called her name.

A further original watercolour on a piece of card measuring 14 x 10 inches is presented in black, whites and greys and shows a man and a woman in Regency costume. They are standing in a wood-panelled room with portraits along the panelling behind them. The gentleman is kissing the lady's hand and is very much in supplicative mode. However this doesn't seem to be a successful venture as the lady is turning her head away and has a distinctly mischievous expression on her face.

The market for high quality beautifully bound books was seriously curtailed by the outbreak of World War One. By this time James and Ruby were married with two children and living at Orchard House, Moresby, near Whitehaven, James had a painting of his daughter, Betty aged 7, accepted by the Royal Academy of Art in 1915 and enlisted in the army during the Autumn of that year. His work took a dramatic turn from magazine and book illustrations to designing and painting stage scenery for *Aladdin, a Pantomime in Two Acts and Eight Gas Attacks* produced by his army unit in Zeneghem in Belgium.

As a final rather lovely footnote to this section of his work, Durden's granddaughter, Janet, possesses a precious copy of *Nina's Career* by Christina Gowans White. It's a hardback first edition published by Henry Frowde and Hodder and Stoughton in 1908. It is illustrated in colour by James Durden, with an illustration on the spine and on the front cover. The pages are gilt-edged. The author has dedicated it to a Mary F.A. Williams, London, 1903-1907, but the dedication that makes this particular volume unique is the black ink handwritten message on the opening page. It simply reads *To Janet from Grandad* with the familiar J Durden signature partway down the page. A precious gift indeed!

29

5: Ruby

Ruby, Betty and James

One of my first reference points for Ruby was to start at the end of her story! After tramping around through some wet grass I located a handsome gravestone tucked away under trees in Crosthwaite churchyard, Keswick. It's quite an unusual shape with a half curve sitting on small shoulders and within that curve there is a simple but attractive motif of three stylised trees within a circular frame. It's striking in its simplicity and design. Round the edge of the circle are the words *IN LOVING MEMORY*. This is the last resting place of Ruby Valentina Durden, born on July 3rd 1877 and who died on April 21st 1958. (Durden's name was added to this headstone on his death in 1964). Ruby Valentina Ellis became Mrs James Durden in July 1907.

This unusual gravestone sits with three other rather grander and taller headstones. These are all the same style with matching features and are connected to various members of the wealthy Ellis family. Next to Ruby and James are Ruby's brother James Valentine Ellis (1874-1935) and his wife Victorine (1877-1955) and then a separate headstone for Lillian Mary Ellis (1882-1936), Ruby's younger sister. The final headstone in the row of four commemorates Ruby's parents Sarah Martha Ellis (1851-1925), beloved wife of Joseph Ellis, who is also featured with his dates (1850-1940). Also on that headstone is Margaret E. Ellis, the wife of younger son Wilfrid. It is interesting to note that Lillian is spelt with double L on her gravestone, so I'm assuming that this is the correct spelling. On the memorial plaque described in Chapter 17, the name only has one L which may have risen from the fact that Ruby often calls her sister Lily.

Sarah Martha's maiden name was Valentine, which explains

Ruby

The Artist's Wife

the family name being given to Ruby and James. The Valentine family were involved in the iron and steel industry in the West Cumberland. The first mention of this background that I could locate comes from a letter from Denise Grice (known as Nessy, Ruby's niece) to Janet in 2003. Here she identifies Uncle Herbert Valentine as being the manager of the Seaton Iron Works at Barepot. She also mentions Uncle Charlie and Uncle Ernest and writes *the men all had connections with the works.*

The Valentines were a successful, industrious and wealthy family. Into this family came Joseph Ellis. The 1851 census records the young Ellis family living with parents-in-law Joseph and Ann Diggle in Saddleworth, Yorkshire. Ben Ellis, born in Saddleworth, was 27 and recorded as a handloom weaver (cotton). His wife Mary Ann Ellis was born in Rochdale in Lancashire and was 29. Their baby was the 3 month old Joseph. With this socio-economic background Joseph appeared destined to tread a familiar track. Nessy writing about her grandfather recalls: *I never heard of any other children after Joseph, but I know he started work at the age of seven. He was a pit head boy and made tea for people in the offices (he would hardly be big enough to lift the kettle!). He must have made good use of his time to be in a position to marry at twenty something.*

There is no record of how the self-made Joseph came to be in Cumberland and in a position to marry the wealthy Sarah

33

Martha Valentine. Their first son, James Valentine Ellis, born in 1874, joined the family firm and pursued a very successful industrial career, but this is another story. Sufficient to say his obituary under the heading *WELL KNOWN WORKINGTON INDUSTRIALIST* opens with the paragraph: *Mr James Valentine Ellis, OBE who died recently in a nursing home in Edinburgh at the age of 60, was chiefly instrumental in securing the building of the Prince of Wales Dock at Workington.* Within one generation the pattern of poverty and drudgery had shifted significantly and Joseph Ellis was surely very proud of his son. The death of this successful son at the age of 60 must have been a bitter blow for his 85 year old father.

> **MARRIAGE OF MISS ELLIS.**
>
> Many friends took part in beautifying our Church with floral decorations on Tuesday, the 30th of July, on the occasion of the marriage of Miss Ruby Valentina Ellis, daughter of Mr. Joseph Ellis, of the Manor House, to Mr. James Durden, son of the late Mr. Durden, of Manchester. The Vicar officiated and Mr. Taylor presided at the organ. The bride was given away by her father and looked very charming in a beautiful gown of oriental satin, trimmed with Bruges lace, chiffon and panne velvet and carrying a handsome bouquet made up of roses, lilies and white heather.
>
> The only bridesmaid was her sister, Miss Lily Ellis, dressed in pale grey and white voile, trimmed with pink panne velvet and lace, and carrying a shower bouquet of pink carnations. Mr. W. E. Webster acted as the bridegroom's best man. A large number of guests attended the reception held after the ceremony at the Manor House and wished "God-speed" to the happy couple as they left, amid a shower of rice, for Cornwall, where the honeymoon was to be spent. At the instigation of a certain little lady, whose name it would scarcely be fair to divulge, the carriage drove away not altogether unadorned on the outside. The numerous presents formed a handsome collection. We understand Mr. and Mrs. Durden have taken a house in Claygate and we take this opportunity of heartily welcoming them to our Parish.

Ruby Valentina Ellis was born in 1877 and her birthplace is given as the coal-mining Ashton under Lyne, in Lancashire. Joseph's fortunes were tied to the successful Valentine family and in 1872 he was involved with foundation of the Moss Bay Hermatite Iron Company. This company became the Workington Iron and Steel Company in 1909. John Randles was the chairman and Joseph Ellis was the managing director. His son Wilfred was also a director and his other son, James Valentine Ellis, was the General Manager. James V. Ellis was in charge when the King visited the works in 1916. His services during the war were recognised with the award of an O.B.E.

In the 1891 census the Ellis family were living at 8, Lorne Villas in Workington. Joseph is described as an 'iron master', son James Valentine is 16 and a 'chemist's assistant', Ruby is 13 and a scholar, Wilfred is 9, Lillian (Lily) is 8.

In the same letter about her family, Nessy (the daughter of

James and Victorine) reports: *There is a strong Manchester connection - my father went to Manchester Grammar School, but they also moved about a lot. It was the fashion to rent houses rather than buy. They must have been near London when he got his ironmaster's qualification and met my mother and the sisters went to the Slade and met Jim Durden.*

Whatever education the Ellis children received in Workington they thrived and it would appear that Ruby was interested in Art and painting. By 1895, according to her niece, she was a student at the Slade. James Durden was at the Royal College of Art. James and Ruby may have met at this time or may have come across each other earlier in Manchester.

In the April, 1901, census, Ruby is shown as a visitor at the home of Alice Palmer in Blenheim Crescent, Kensington. Ruby is now 23 and has either never left London or has possibly returned as a visitor.

In 1901 James is lodging in Putney, in 71 Chelverton Road, with the family of his old friend Walter Webster.

However much time Ruby spent with James in the Spring of 1901, the situation had changed by the following year. The Ellis family were now residing at Langfield House at 37, The High Street, Workington. Joseph was Managing Director of the ironworks. Wilfrid at 19, is a clerk in the ironworks, Lillian is still at home at 18 and there is a last child, a son, John Anthony Arnold aged 8, has arrived. The family seem to be doing well.

In 1902 Ruby is on a Caribbean cruise and she is writing to James, who is now residing at Jubilee Place in Chesea. The chapter called *Darling Heart* looks at these letters in detail and it is obvious that no separation is going to compromise Ruby's feelings for James.

Cards and letters are addressed to James as he moves around. Ruby goes away on a second cruise this time to the West Indies. A letter goes to 78, Lynwood Road, Blackburn. In 1905 a card to James from Ruby is addressed to Pomona House, Kings Road, Fulham. Ruby is back home in Workington in 1906, but the whole romance comes to fruition on July 30th 1907 when James Durden bachelor marries Ruby Valentina Ellis spinster at

Holy Trinity Church, Claygate in Surrey. The Ellis family had left Workington to live in an impressive detached house with 10 bedrooms called The Manor House on Beaconsfield Road in Claygate. Holy Trinity church is a beautiful old parish church with two towers and a lovely lych-gate entrance. The two witnesses at the wedding are James' old friends of Manchester and Putney days, Walter Ernest Webster and Thomas Dugdale. Lily, Ruby's sister is the bridesmaid. On the copy of the marriage certificate in the Army records, Joseph Ellis is also given as a witness. The marriage was solemnised by the then vicar Allen Barrett.

It appears to have been quite a big wedding with *a large number of guests* and a *reception held after the ceremony at the Manor House.* The Claygate Parish Magazine described the wedding outfits and offered some delightful detail about the departure of the carriage *not altogether unadorned on the outside as* the couple leave for a honeymoon in Cornwall. Lily is obviously the instigator and described as *the certain little lady, whose name it would be scarcely fair to divulge.*

Mr and Mrs James Durden start their married life at 'Redcot', Vale Road, Claygate. The arrival of their first child, a little girl, takes place the following year on June 3rd, 1908. She is taken back to the beautiful parish church of Holy Trinity, where her parents were married the previous year and on the 12th July 1908 she is baptised by the same vicar, Allen Barrett. Gone are the references to the maiden name of her maternal grandmother. There is no Valentina this time and not even the addition of a second name.

The new baby is simply christened Betty.

6: Darling Heart

During January 1902, two letters arrived at 8, Jubilee Terrace, Kings Road, Chelsea addressed to 'Jas Durden'. They were from Ruby. They were written in pencil on rather flimsy paper, but they are still legible. James and Ruby were seeing each other in the Spring of 1901, but now Ruby is seriously in love with James and missing him dreadfully.

Four more letters have survived to the present day and these are dated December 1902. The tone is the same. Ruby's love letters are an interesting mix of lively descriptions and observations about her surroundings, her maladies and heartbreak at the enforced separation from her *own darling boy*..

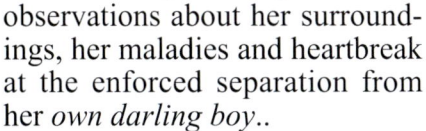

On both occasions Ruby and James are separated because Ruby is on board the Steam Yacht 'Argonaut' on a cruise *"to educate and inform passengers"* (The Argonaut owned by Henry Lunn boasted accommodation for 120 passengers and 120 crew. There was a large refrigerated food store, electric lighting, new boilers and quadruple expansion engines. Guests were invited to enjoy first class on board facilities with wonderful food and a programme of concerts and lectures. The

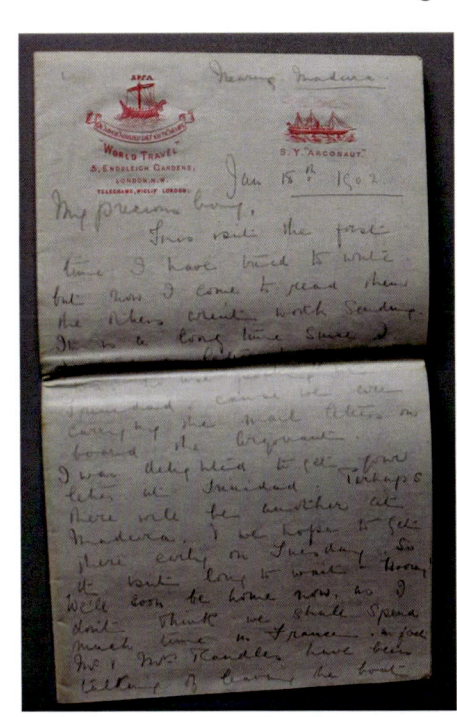

On Deck Letter

promenade deck was spacious enough to play cricket or quoits and there were plenty of opportunities for exercise. All of Ruby's letters, with the exception of one from a hotel stay, are written on the ship's cream notepaper with the 'World Travel' crest in embossed red lettering with a little illustration of the Argonaut

This was luxury travel in 1902 and there is no doubt that Ruby enjoyed her time on board and the opportunity to travel to far distant climes. A contemporary photograph taken during the Argonaut's heyday shows a jolly group of (nearly) smiling passengers gathered on the top deck and apparently having fun.

Ruby's enjoyment was somewhat compromised, on occasions, by severe seasickness and the unpredictability of collecting post from home (actually, from Jimmy), at various ports and her irritation at times when trying to write letters to him. She appears to have tried to sit on deck to write and gets quite cross when various fellow travellers interrupt her activity by attempting to join her and chat. Separation from James dominates all her letters and there's real heartbreak when post from London fails to deliver the longed for letter from Jubilee Place.

The letters follow the same format with the writing paper being presented in a double folded sheet. Ruby writes the first page and then goes to the back to what logically should be page 4. Pages 3 and 4 feature in the middle of the folded sheet with extra single pages added in if necessary. Sometimes pages are numbered, but not always and there are time lapses especially if sea-sickness intervenes!

Ruby is not with her family but she is accompanied by her twenty year old sister Lily (Lillian) and her parents' friends, Mr and Mrs Randles, later to become Sir John and Lady Randles. Sir John was another iron and steel magnate.

Ruby went on two separate cruises on the 'Argonaut', one in January 1902 in the Mediterranean and one in December 1902 when letters come from the Caribbean.

The two letters from the Mediterranean were written towards the end of the cruise and describe various incidents from the preceding few weeks. However the accounts are rather overtaken by the excitement about getting home and the prospect of arriving in

London and seeing James again. These two letters are also accompanied by a series of sepia snapshots. Fortuitously, Ruby has written the destinations on the back of the pictures (well done Ruby). Some feature her travelling companions and on occasions Ruby herself with further observations *a terrible one of me.*

On January 18th,1902, she is n*earing Madeira* and hopes to get there *"early on Tuesday"*. She hasn't heard from James since she collected a letter in Trinidad and is hoping to find another one in Madeira. She is also anticipating the rest of the journey: *I don't think we'll spend much time in France* but *if we keep to time we are going to have a few hours in Gibraltar - won't that be jolly?* This is followed by a detailed description of recent time spent in Martinique where there had been a volcanic eruption. In fact the St Pierre volcano was still active so going ashore was seen by the passengers as a dangerous, risky and exciting business: *whilst we were on shore an eruption took place which would have killed us all had the wind been in the opposite direction.* She describes walking on bones which were everywhere and picks up some relics but obviously felt a bit uncomfortable about it: *I found some lace partly burned of course - and embroidery satin, part of the priest's vestments in the cathedral and bits of prayerbooks. A little black boy came over with them and had picked up a carving which I gave him a dollar for ....*

There seems to be an adventurous feeling to such a risky business and she points out that the local newspaper called them 'Mad English Tourists'.

Dominica provided a much more pleasant experience. The men on board had a cricket match against a native team in a beautiful park and she adds that she would have liked to stay there much longer.

Sea sickness now intervenes but she continues from her 'little bunk' the following day (19th January). The boat is described as *wobbling from side to side most horribly.* Dinner has been an experience when *all the things on the table did a war dance. Lily's bottle of ginger ale - we always drink it when we feel at all bad - flew under the central table in the room leaving a stream all the way and then back again right up to the top of* ours yet when she picked it up there was still some left in it. It's very exciting at Mealtimes!*

Activities on board are described with the men's obstacle race being seen as *very funny* but the men too are victims of the rolling conditions. She says some of them *have been in bed all day and seem to take it in turns.*

It would appear that she is beginning to get a bit bored and regrets not bringing any work *if you've something to do you don't notice the movement so much.* Mrs Randles comes to her rescue and lends her some crochet work. She completes a doyley and begins another one.

All this is interspersed with her longing to see James: *I want to see my darling boy so much, I can think of nothing else now Jimmy - it's a terribly long time since I felt you near me. I want to snuggle up into your waistcoat.*

The Argonaut reached Madeira at 4:30 pm on the 20th January. Ruby thinks they have missed the post, but she signs it off in case it can be posted. Her *"bye bye sweetheart"* is followed by an affectionate *with all Babbie's love.*

Ruby observes that Madeira looks *a jolly Place from my porthole* but sadly she is met with a setback on arrival. There is no letter from James! She describes it as a *horrible disappointment, especially as there are other letters from England.*

The little party really enjoy Madeira: *the climate is lovely and so is the place.* They participate in the popular tourist activity of going up the mountain by train and after lunch coming down in the traditional toboggan *like wildfire.* She says she would like to return and assures James he would love the mountain experience. She's also bought him a little replica of the traditional carriage transport drawn by two bullocks. She is really appreciative of the pleasant and mild climate as they have been feeling cold after leaving the tropics. Amusingly she writes that: *this would be quite summer weather in Workington.*

The next letter starts *My Dear Jimmy* and was dated January 23rd 1902 and now the location is off Gibraltar. Much of this letter is concerned with the arrangements for the ongoing journey and Ruby's excitement is building. It appears that the Randles have decided to push through France (presumably this is the disembarkation point for all passengers?) and arrive in London on Wednesday afternoon. There is some conjecture about how she and Lily will manage their luggage and she is obviously torn between not having enough time to see Paris properly but delighted to be *seeing my boy all the sooner.*

The boat is due in Gibraltar the following day and will leave at 3 pm giving the passengers a brief chance to look round and then they are heading for Marseilles. At this point, Ruby shows some concern about the logistics of not being in time to catch the day train and possibly travelling by night and only getting an hour and a half in Paris.

In one paragraph during this letter she apologises for the disconnection in the structure of her letters. *I can't help it. There are people all around and first one and then another come and talk to me and I forget where I am. I'm writing with this on my knee and no book so it's difficult.*

What was probably the culmination of the Sports Programme has taken place with prizes distributed by Mrs Randles. Lily has won two prizes, one for bucket quoits and the other as part of a bean bags team. However, by the awards evening Lily is *seedy and has to stay in bed* so Ruby collects the prizes for her sister.

There is also an amusing description of a rather untraditional cricket match featuring the ladies against the gentlemen. The fun arises from the fact that the gentlemen wore ladies attire and Ruby writes *Oh how we laughed to be sure. Some of the men cut such funny figures, especially one who wore two curlers in his front hair and a huge bustle that wobbled when he played. Horrible wasn't it?*

In between all this Ruby is trying to do a little packing, before the boat hits troubled waters, but she is struggling with the confines of the cabin. She finishes the letter with the anticipation once again of getting back: *Hooray - London on Wednesday - it is jolly to think we are so near. You didn't expect me back so soon,did you sweetheart. Mr and Mres Randles will go to Workington on Thursday or Friday. I hope I shan't have to*

41

go too. Perhaps Mother will be in London to meet us - I hope so.

She signs off *yours always* and adds a cheery little: *PS Night-night Jimmy dear - pleasant dreams.*

There is now a time lapse of nearly a year before Ruby and James are once again separated by the seas. It would appear that a cruise on the S Y Argonaut is a feature of Christmas for the Randles and once again they are accompanied by the Ellis daughters, Ruby and Lily.

One virtually indecipherable letter is started *Darling Heart*. It's undated but the location is described as just off Fayah and postmarked Gibraltar on the 12th December and London on the 16th. The first page is written in ink, but it looks as if it may not be Ruby as it doesn't look like her writing. Did she dictate it to Lily? She has been dreadfully seasick and maybe this is the reason *can only send love - can't write dear - been awfully rough . . . weak . . . feeding on a few biscuits . . . no more sea trips for pleasure for me.*

The rest of this letter is in her normal writing, but it is so faded that only odd phrases and half sentences emerge. The party have been on shore where she says she feels she is a different creature. She manages a *fairly respectable lunch* which appears to be the first proper food for a while. She knows how James will appreciate the vivid colours everywhere and enthuses about the orange groves and hydrangeas *in masses along the roads*. She describes herself as falling in love with *the sweet children with such clear blue eyes.*

After this, two other letters are preserved in the same flimsy envelope postmarked Havana and then with a further postmark as at least one of these letters is forwarded from Jubilee Terrace to 78 Lynwood Road, Preston Road, Blackburn, where James must be spending Christmas.

A second Darling Heart letter is long and appears to have been written as the boat crossed on the outward voyage towards the Azores heading for the Caribbean. This one is really difficult to read and some parts are simply so faded as to be completely obscured. She continues to be very sea sick and says: *"It has been awful with a capital A* adding that *I have only had one day without seasickness,* describing the boat as a *fearful roller*. They have also had 10 days of *fearful weather which ended in a dreadful storm . . . one of our boats disappeared and I believe a photograph was taken. . . The pitching and tossing has obviously taken its toll on the boat as well as the passengers, the damage has been tremendous . . . I forget how many hundreds of plates have been broken.*

At one point she does attempt to go down to dinner and describes how *forks, plates and food slipped all over the place and looked disgusting, but in spite of it all it was so ridiculous one couldn't help laughing. You can't realise at what an angle the boat can go over yet right itself again.* She continues *so many have been hurt being thrown out of their berths. Yesterday I saw a snapshot of myself with others on the hurricane deck taken on one of the worst days. It looks like the photograph of patients at a convalescent home.*

She comments that ten days is a long time to be away from land and every sign of life and points out that even *the seagulls have left us.* It then looks as if the situation gradually improves (does she get her sea legs?) and she writes *it is wonderful what a difference a still day makes to the passengers. Most of them have been talking about going home from the next stopping place by most wonderful routes - anything but rolling home in the Argonaut. They seem more resigned today - one man is in a dreadful weak state yet - I have felt so sorry for him.*

With more time to observe her seascape surroundings she tells James about the flying fish, adding that: *Miss Iredale has got one in her cabin which she intends to have preserved the stewardess knows how to do it.* She describes the seaweed as *very pretty with great masses of it on top of the water, it looks as though tons of tobacco had been upset.*

There is an amusing incident when: *Mr Randles and a few others thought they had discovered an octopus and immediately there was a crowd hanging over the side of the ship. It looks very wriggly said one. In a minute another said it looks like vegetables and then up came a turkey's head and then some feathers and the octopus turned out to be from the turkey's inside, and skin.*

43

The other hazard of this long crossing from the Azores to the Caribbean was the possibility of the boat being caught in high winds and Ruby appears to have had a narrow escape from a nasty accident one night. She had opted out of dinner and was on deck by herself even though it is f*earfully wild*. She goes on: *the sail got loose and began to flap about creating a noise like thunder. I couldn't make out what was the matter cause it seems as though the whole (boat?) was going over. When I saw a sailor rush to the end of the ship I had to get out of my chair, but I was so weak - had never tried to walk by myself that I immediately fell on my face. How I managed to crawl to the saloon door I don't know, but I did it on hands and knees. Just as I got there the whole sail came down about where I was sitting. I felt quite terrified and some of the men rushed up from the dinner table in a great flap.*

Some social activities resumed. She managed to dress for dinner one night and, feeling better, went to the Fancy Dress Ball which she says she quite enjoyed. She's probably aware of James' interest in costume and explains: *The costumes were quite presentable, considering what some of them had to work on. There were prizes given. I took photographs of the costumes yesterday - the prize winners and some others took the trouble to dress again on purpose.*

She didn't manage to put together a costume for herself, but described the winners: *The performance prize went to* (indecipherable name)*, dressed as Mother's Darling with a white frock and sash. Lily had them. He carried a weird looking doll - he acted the part splendidly. The Prize Lady looked very sweet . . . I hope the snapshot I took of her comes out well. 'An Early Victorian Lady' she called herself and she had one of the Fayal hats trimmed into a bonnet most beautifully.* Within the next indistinct lines she seems to indicate that the best costumes are those procured on land. One particular one is a man dressed as *a Russian Jew and was so realistic. I shuddered when he came near me - so did most people. He is a very nice man - so kindly.*

There is a dry reference to: *the stewards gave a concert last night - they enjoyed themselves whether other people did or not.*

The Argonaut then encountered another spell of stormy

weather and with some fortitude poor Ruby attempted to see the funny side of it all: *Teapots, coffee pots, cruet sets, cushions, books, oranges, in fact everything simply got mixed up and crashed from one end of the saloon to the other. The piano jumped up and down although supposed to be tied up securely. Our boxes and chairs in our cabins, my clothes and loose articles played hide and seek the whole time. We just spent time trying to stick in our berths. The boat was first at this angle and then round the other way.*

There is some description of the recent shore stop in Fayah (in the Azores). Although not very impressed with the place, she does describe an interesting encounter in the Cathedral where they were just in time for a christening: *the way the priest pulled that unfortunate baby about was awful. At the end of the ceremony Mr Randles presented the baby with a threepenny piece with a hole with string through and after the priest had blessed it or taken it of course I don't know which - it was tied onto the baby and worn for luck.*

Interspersed with all this news is the constant theme of how much Ruby is missing James and wanting to know how he is getting on: *Have you finished the drawing of kiddies in costumes? I hope the editors are being kind to you dear and keeping you busy so you won't feel lonely. Has Tommy begun the portrait yet?*

I wonder what you have been doing since I left. Oh what a long time it seems to have to wait for news. Anything could happen in the time. Keep well and cheerful Jimmy dear. If this letter is not what you expected please forgive me. It is written under such difficulties. Lily is trying to write and has to ask how to spell every other word nearly. We ought to be in Nassau by now. We shall spend one day less there cause we are late. Perhaps we shall sight land this evening, but we don't expect to land there until tomorrow afternoon.

It's signed off the next morning: *Nassau is in sight and we expect to lunch at 12 o'clock and then go ashore. I'm positively ashamed to send this letter which I can't even read over. A whale has been seen this morning. Lily and I went on deck at 7:30 but were too late to see it.*

45

Toboggan Tracks in Madeira

Bye bye Darling - don't quite forget your little girl. She would give anything to see your dear face today. Here comes the pilot - every-one is getting very excited. If I can write a little about Nassau I will.

With all ? . . . And love
Enjoy yourself at Xmas time dear. Please give my love to your mother and sister.

(This last greeting suggests that James spent Christmas with his sister Edith Cockbain, at 78 Lynwood Road, Manchester.)

Ruby does manage to give James some very brief information about Nassau in the next letter written in Cuba. She is devastated to find no letter from James awaiting her in Nassau and she has a fearful headache on the sightseeing drive round that area.

The next letter in the Christmas week envelope is still on Argonaut writing paper, but is now written in black ink, making it much easier to decipher! This one starts *My Dear Laddie* and was written as the boat reached Cuba. The previous day an early lunch had been taken and the party had disembarked for a trip to Havana. In true cruise fashion transport (an electric car) has been organised and guides are provided. The Randle group appears to have had their own independent guide.

Ruby described the tourist highlights of the trip taken over a few days, a cigar factory, a pineapple grove and a sugar plantation. She tried to get photographs of the *lovely girls* working at the cigar factory, but met with little success: *they don't like being photographed and turned their backs on us.* The party is taken by train and electric car to a pineapple grove where they sample the fruit and find it 'delicious' and marvel at the banana palms. She appreciates their *'jolly good guide* apparently organised by the Randles and comments that *it is so nice to keep away from the crowds.* Later in this letter she describes a

Bullock cart

grapefruit as *a cross between an orange and a lemon and rather bitter but rather nice.*
The sugar plantation was reached after driving over some very bumpy roads, but the workers were only there six months of the year and the machinery would not operating until the following month, so this attraction was deemed to be *uninteresting and anyway very dirty.*

In some ways nothing changes as the highlights of these sightseeing shore visits also featured lunches out and shopping. Hotel Inglatera is a popular stop and she records a lunch one day: O*h how we enjoyed it - we laughed until we were quite foolish.*

Shopping was a rather puzzling experience . . . the vendors are described as *fearful rogues* and the currency as *so perplexing. Somebody paid 16/- for a pair of gloves and was asked 30/- for a straw hat which wasn't even trimmed.*

There is a brief mention of a visit to Nassau with a long sightseeing drive, but Ruby's *fearful headache* impacted on that particular outing and initially there is no further comment apart from *fairly interesting.* However when the passengers start looking round the town the situation improved and she saw the streets as *quaint.* She's impressed with the natives' ability to speak such good English and then goes on to comment on the Spanish influence in Havana. Here Spanish was spoken and she admired the dresses and mantillas worn by the girls with their *languishing eyes.*

Social activities on board continued with *another dance the night before last* but plainly this was not really the sort of energetic activity to be pursued in tropical heat. Her observation here foud the word *"warm"* somewhat inadequate and she moves to *we nearly melted.*

As ever James and contact with him was the top priority and he doesn't appear to be a very responsive correspondent. No letter arrived with the rest of the post in Nassau, although other letters from home were there. She was bitterly disappointed and rationalized the situation to herself about the American liners being delayed by the storm and some mail being 3 days late. She was desperate to hear from him and there was a slight anxiety coming through . . . *Don't quite forget your little girl will you Jimmy?* She is very reassuring about her loyalty to him. *There is no one to come near my boy on this boat. I want him here so badly.* She says she will think of him on Thursday (which is Christmas Day) and will try to imagine him in Blackburn adding that she *would love to spend Christmas with you, sweetheart.*

The picture postcard of Havana is also written on December 19th. It got to Chelsea and then to Blackburn byJanuary 3rd 1903. It shows a wide cobbled street, Calle Obispo, and was possibly one of the main shopping areas with pavements, attractive buildings and a few pedestrians. There was only space for a brief comment and she is surprisingly circumspect *Isn't this New: Year card pretty? Good wishes from R.* It would seem that she is aware that this particular message might be seen by other eyes!

Ruby continued to write to James at length during all that Christmas week and a letter started to Jimmy Dear on board on December 23rd is concluded in the comfort of the Constant Spring Hotel near Kingston Jamaica on the 26th December. She reported the changes to the itinerary as apparently not enough time has been allowed for some shore visits. St Kitts and Barbados were now off the list and she was very disappointed not to get to St Kitts. A brief stop at Cien-fuego was dismissed as *not a nice place* but it had given them the opportunity to buy some pineapples for 3d each.

There are several references in the letters to the ship's artist, Mr Tristram Ellis. His surname appears to be coincidental. Ruby attempted to record events with her camera and tried to get a photograph of him painting. In what she considered to be a very amusing incident she came across *a crowd gath-*

Marseilles

"... awful one of me in Nassau"

ered at what she takes to be a prayer meeting only to have discovered Mr Ellis in the middle trying to paint. She said she would call the photo 'Our Artist in Difficulties!' She writes a little about the photographs. She has had some film developed and thinks she might send some photos to James. (In fact she did just that and he kept photographs which are still in the archive.) She bemoaned her lack of photo-graphic skills and wished she had practised a little more before the voyage. Obviously some anticipated pictures had seriously gone awry and she says *Few of them have nothing on and a few dark specks and I don't know the reason.*

She was still beset by too much company on deck with 5 visitors *pouring out their woes to me about mosquito bites and other rubbish!. . . .* She was really irritated!

The ever threatening seasickness was still present of course, but she had now learnt to combat it a little by eating 'petite fours'.

However the main excitement of this letter is the anticipation of landing at Port Antonio in Jamaica the following day and going overland to spend Christmas Day at the Constant Spring Hotel near Kingston in Jamaica.

This last surviving letter starting *My Own Darling Boy* was written on December 26th from the hotel. Although supposedly a continuation of the one on board, it is a very different epistle to most of the rest of the correspondence. It would appear that several factors were involved. For a start she's on terra firma which is much appreciated . . .

It was so nice to feel a still bed under us for once. And of course it's Christmas, so no doubt the Hotel did everything possible to help their clients celebrate the festive season so far away from home.

However the real Christmas present arrived in the post in the form of a letter from James. At last! She had been really distressed initially when there was nothing from James *yesterday or this morning* and described herself as *very unhappy and not*

49

very well. However more post had arrived later in the day and she suspected that some letters may have been lost at the Havana stop. Towards the end of this long letter she responded to him

Dear you were a darling for writing such a sweet letter. I shall go to bed and dream sweet dreams tonight - without opium. I wonder if you know I'm thinking of you now. It seems funny to think you are dreaming now probably. It will be between 2 and 3 o'clock in the morning in England.

Sweetheart I can't say such nice things as you do. I want to but they won't come. I want to tell you how dear you are to me. It has been a long month without any news from you. I want my boy so badly at times. I want you always dear. Of course I think of that little home we are going to share some day. When will it be I wonder dear. Oh Jimmy I don't want to leave you ever.

The letter also contains her descriptions of her Christmas trips. The boat arrived at Port Antonio on the morning of Christmas Eve and part of the party immediately disembarked for a drive to the tourist attraction known as the Blue Hole. They drove passed a market on the road and she marvels at the women carrying all their provisions home in bundles on their heads *they seem to walk for miles and miles very heavily laden.* They were caught in heavy tropical rain, but this doesn't seem to have affected her appreciation of the Blue Hole and the vivid blue mountains. She comments that *this is a lovely place - very like the Lake District only of course the vegetation is quite different.*

They spend the night at a hotel in Port Antonio. Her little excursion party is up very early on Christmas morning for another exciting trip on their way to the Constant Spring Hotel. Some passengers have stayed on the ship until they arrived in Kingston, but it appears the more intrepid travellers have done this extra night in St Antonio and then taken an overland train journey. It's still raining, but she enjoys the scenery.

They join the rest of the passengers in the hotel by lunchtime but then sadly Ruby is overtaken by *a complaint, very common in this part of the world.* She obviously wants to spare James the details, but has to retire to bed and be dosed with opium. This problem is supposed to last for twelve hours and she is very grateful to be on land! She spends the rest of Christmas Day observing the splendid bedroom and the verandah they have all to themselves. They are well protected with mosquito nets but she watches the lizards (looks like lugards but must be lizards!) crawl in and out of the lattice work in the balcony. These don't seem to bother her but she's less enthusiastic about the ants swarming all over the floor and even in the waterhole and flush (where she obviously spent some time!) Some of the rest of the party go to a Dance that night to the Myrtle Hotel, but not Ruby.

However she seems to be much recovered by Boxing Day morning and goes on the drive to Hope Garden and then onto a garden town. She is still fit enough to go to Kingston in an electric car after lunch to a Fair of some sort and admires the black girls with their spectacular neck sleeves. *They have beautiful faces and carry themselves beautifully with lovely dresses*. The party also went to a *kind of Minstrel performance, but soon came away it wasn't up to much.* She hopes to do some shopping in Kingston the following day before they leave after dinner.

She gives James some news from her other letters . . . her friend Edith (is this her sister in law?) and her brother Wilfrid *is getting fat in America.* She refers to the Indian Summer he is having out there and hopes it won't get much hotter on board the Argonaut as *I couldn't very well take off more clothes.*

She comments that she is hoping to meet Geoffrie and Daisy at Port of Spain. This is in Trinidad and probably refers to the family she lodged with in London in April 1901. Alice Palmer, the owner of the Blenheim Crescent House was born in Trinidad and Daisy Riddel, her niece was also born in Trinidad. The unknown G is described as *a dear old girl* who is elated at the prospect of seeing them.

The last section of the letter is concerned with the natural world around them, particularly the environs of the Blue Hole. There she drank cocoa-nut milk from the green nuts and tasted the nut part when jelly. She enjoys the oranges, pineapples and bananas but doesn't like the plantains and ruefully acknowledges she has over indulged with the fruit. The butterflies and hummingbirds are much appreciated .

Reference to her sickness makes her slightly anxious about staying healthy as obviously this is supposed to be one of the main benefits of an ocean cruise: *All the time through that awful seasickness I kept cheering myself up by thinking how much good this trip was going to do me cause the better I am in health the happier I shall be able to make you some day.*

She doesn't want James to get tired of such a seasick looking girl, so finally, *Goodnight Darling . . . sweet dreams of me and a nice little kiss from your girlie x.*

These letters have photographs enclosed, so James can see the places she is describing. Originally black and white and measuring about 3x2 inches, they are now a sepia colour and somewhat faded, but relatively clear. To her everlasting credit Ruby has written the locations on the back in pencil. She refers to her lack of photographic skills on several occasions through the corres-pondence, but as holiday snaps they are pretty impressive. The most useful are the ones where she has identified people and it's a joy to see the Randles, Lily and on several occasions Ruby herself. She has obviously relinquished the camera at times!

There are twenty photographs of the December 1902 voyage. *An awful one of myself at Nassau* shows a slim and attractive young lady in fashionable Edwardian garb with a long sleeved ruffled blouse and a long skirt. She looks the typical efficiently equipped tourist with a lovely hat, parasol and a good sized leather shoulder bag carried in front. She is smiling at a passing native man and looks delightful. I love this picture. There is one of Lily watching washerwomen at St Lucia in a similar outfit with the parasol opened. The Cienfuegos picture of Tristram Ellis is included but mostly of the crowd as opposed to the artist himself. A better one of Mr Ellis shows him sketching rather a spectacular view of a bay in St Lucia with Lily and a fellow passenger, Mr Walker watching proceedings. Drinks have been provided. The markets and street scenes in Havana are shown and there is an interesting one of the Customs House and landing stage there. In the market place in Dominica, goods for sale just sit on the cobbled street with vendors in attendance. In two photos we can see the transport used to taxi visitors around. Both The Blue Hole at Port Antonio and the Pineapple grove show horse drawn carriages with a distinctly Victorian appearance. Ruby doesn't appear to have taken many photos on board the ship, but there is one taken from the deck of the sea below. It's labelled as *boys diving for money at Nassau* and shows a canoe type craft with three occupants poised to participate in this lucrative game.

The pictures are a fascinating backup to Ruby's letters and illustrate her travel writing most effectively. Well done Ruby and a special round of applause for writing a location on the back of every single one. James is going to know exactly where she is travelling.

The same pattern is repeated with the closing stages of the earlier January 1902 cruise featured at the beginning of this chapter. 16 photographs were sent home in Letter number One to *My Precious Boy* and Letter number Two to *My Dear Jimmy*, again all thankfully labelled. The volcanic activity at St Pierre on Martinique obviously made an impression and there are seven pictures of Mont Pelee and the destruction caused. Two of the photos show Ruby standing in front of the ruins and eruption, but in both she is rather indistinct. A better print features Lily. Also amongst the ruins is a picture of a French policeman sent out to supervise their expe-dition. On the back of one she identifies the ruins of the cathedral and describes how *oh so many people* were crowded in there when the eruption took place, they were found *stand-ing up and packed like sardines - all smothered of course*. Three pictures of Pompeii are featured, a coast scene of Capri and three of Madeira. One shows the very recognisable traditional Toboggan used for the run back down to Funchal, the bullock drawn carriage and the tram lines in the cobbled streets. A rather interesting one of Marseilles shows a group of French nurses, but sadly they

53

all have their backs to the camera.

So Ruby does her very best to keep James updated whilst away from him. I'm grateful for the rather voyeurist view of her feelings as exposed in her letters. Plainly if anything goes wrong with this relationship she will be truly heartbroken and I'm really sorry not to ever catch a glimpse of his replies. It seems strange that Ruby's letters survived because James kept them but there is no evidence of Ruby keeping her replies from James which must have been very precious. Maybe he didn't write as many letters!

Whatever happened during the next few years, this relationship survived, and one can only imagine how very very happy Ruby must have been on the morning of July 30th 1907 when she married her precious boy at Holy Trinity Church in Claygate, Surrey.

Interestingly the story of the Argonaut wasn't quite over and I was fascinated to locate a headline in the Los Angeles Herald STEAM YACHT SINKS - IS HIT BY STEAMER with the following information ... The tourist steam yacht Argonaut which left London yesterday bound for Lisbon with 250 persons on board, including passengers and crew, went down between Dover and Dungenness this morning after having been in collision withe steamer Kingswell in a fog. All on board the Argonaut took to the boats and came ashore here in safety.

It's interesting to conjecture whether news of this disaster reached Ruby. If so she was probably hugely relieved to have left her cruising days behind. She is now busy with her 15 week old baby and securely ensconced in her first home as Mrs Durden. This is the house and the life she dreamed of sharing with her own darling boy, whilst sitting on the deck of the 'Argonaut' and writing those heartfelt letters all those years ago.

7: Two Paintings in the Summer of 1915

The two paintings side by side

In 1915 the Durdens were living at Orchard House in Moresby, just outside Whitehaven. James was still working on his book and magazine commissions. Fortunately the family now had the benefit of financial support from Ruby's independent means.

The situation in Europe was worsening by the day and the war that was supposed to be 'over by Christmas' was going badly. James must have been increasingly aware of the 'Your Country Needs You' posters and the pressure to join up. However, he didn't enlist until 30th November, 1915.

During the preceding summer he submitted a painting of Betty on her seventh birthday, to the Royal Academy. It received national recognition and critical acclaim. It shows a lovely child, regarding her doll in a solemn way. She is standing in profile and there is a hint of an imaginary conversation going on between child and precious doll.

The little girl is beautifully dressed in a fashionable frock of the time with a low waist emphasised by a broad ribbon and a bow at the back. The dress falls to knee length in pleated frills below the hip line. The child has a very attractive profile and her short bobbed hair is adorned with a high ribbon. One strand of the elaborate bow falls towards Betty's forehead and a few strands of hair show on her cheek, exposing one ear. She is a little girl absorbed in her own imaginary world. To the right of the child is a long sweep of heavy fabric curtain and in front of her is small low table covered by the same material. On this table is another doll and between Betty and the table is a toy cat on four wheels.

It's a delightful picture and shows the beginning of a life-

Betty aged seven

time of painting Betty. The Newcastle Journal of May 5th 1915 said the picture *has a quiet humour all of its own and of a kind inseparable from childhood and the nursery.* Durden continued to paint Betty until her marriage in 1933 when she left England. These family portraits with their characteristic bold use of colour and form will contrast with his landscapes and become a feature of his growing reputation.

Durden painted another very different picture during that summer of 1915. It is unlike any other painting. It illustrates a surprising and totally unanticipated incident that occurred on August 16th. Whitehaven was at the heart of a thriving industrial area. A large chemical works was situated on the hill near Lowca and Parton villages. The works had been purchased in 1908 by three gentlemen called Randles, Ellis and Burnyeat. Sir John Randles lived in a splendid house, Bristowe Hill in Keswick and used some of his wealth to benefit Keswickians. The Ellis family lived next door in Skiddaw Lodge. William John Dalzell Burnyeat was the local MP. In 1911 the works became the United Coke and Chemical Company, manufacturing toluene, later TNT, for producing explosives.

At dawn, on the morning of August 16th, a German submarine, U boat 24, surfaced about a mile off the coast below Lowca and Parton. It was seen by the harbour master, Captain Cowley and his assistant Robert Moore who were out fishing. It was armed with six torpedoes and a deck gun for firing shells. Its mission was to destroy the Lowca works. The villagers of Parton were woken from their beds by the sound of German shells and fled from their cottages and farms. In Whitehaven, spectators on the piers jeered at the onslaught and applauded if a shell missed the target. The situation was rescued by one Oscar Ohison, whose ingenuity and quick thinking saved the day. He was the valve operator on the works that morning. Half way through the bombardment he set fire to some tar and chemicals, releasing a cloud of fire and smoke. The Germans assumed they had hit their target, but continued to fire shells, this time at the homes of the locals instead. The Stationmaster at Parton, William Twentyman, held the train to Whitehaven at the station,

57

The German Submaribe Attack: Coke Ovens on Fire at Harrington
Beacon Museum, Whitehaven

The Lowca Works Bombardment
Janet Durden-Hey

explaining to the passengers that if they proceeded on the journey, they would be shelled by a German U-boat. The submariners slipped away congratulating themselves on the (mistaken) knowledge of mission accomplished.

Little damage was done. One house took a direct hit. The only casualty was a farm dog called Lion and the villagers turned him into a martyr. A commemorative poster was produced headed *In Immortal Memory to Lion, a faithful English Dog.* The poster also honoured *Sandy A timid little mouse* and *Patrick a little chirping sparrow,* who were described as the victims of *German Hun Kultur.* The German press, in contrast, hailed the incident as a *Heroic and Successful Raid on the Enemy's War effort.*

Joseph Holmes (1859-1930), a Stationmaster on the Lowca Line wrote a poem *The Bombardment of the Cumberland Coast* highlighting the event in a mock-heroic style. Public-spiritedly, he sold the poem on handbills for one penny with proceeds *given to the Soldiers Tobacco Fund.*

A post card commemorating the event was identified in Ron Bell's 'Copeland Crack'. It shows the location of the attack and where the shells fell, with the heading 'The latest in Germ-Hun frightfulness' by 'Hun Pirates' on the 'undefended Cumberland Coast'.

Living in Moresby. it's likely that the Durdens witnessed the events of that surprising morning. James's painting shows the works in dramatic silhouette through the inferno of flames engulfing them against a smoke filled sky. In the top corner a branch of a tree shows but also seems to have got caught in the flames as some leaves appear to be falling in a charred and burned state. It is completely different to any other Durden painting and gives a spectacular and accurate graphic representation of the attack.

The Lowca picture took on a life of its own. Janet thinks that it was exhibited in Keswick, but at some point it was confiscated by the authorities as a "sensitive" subject. It was returned after the war and remained in the family going from artist to son Joseph and to granddaughter Janet. It moved with the family from Keswick to the south of England, to Canada, to the U.S.A. and

60

back to England and finally to Scotland. It now has pride of place in Janet Durden-Hey's home on the Isle of Skye.

Another version of this painting, called *The German Submarine Attack,* came into the Beacon Museum in Whitehaven in 1982. Janet Durden-Hey brought her grandfather's painting down from Skye and, on a very sunny 19th May, 2022, Alex Milner, Curator of the Beacon, kindly accommodated our request to bring their painting out of the Art store. The Beacon Museum's painting of the Bombardment at Lowca was brought into the room and we were finally able to view the paintings side by side.

The pictures were virtually identical though the family painting was slightly larger, (68 x 50cm) as opposed to the Beacon version (63 x 45cm). Some slight differences showed up with the details of the tree/leaf patterns in the top right hand corner of the pictures. The heavy ornate gilt Beacon frame was appropriate but rather badly fitted and the canvas appeared a little loose. Both pictures carried the same signature with a slight curve to the customary single surname Durden (although not enclosed in the rectangular box). The paint in the Beacon's Durden looked a little thinner than the oils in the family version, but Janet and I both felt that was little doubt that Durden painted this particular scene twice.

The family picture has been in the possession of the Durden family since the end of World War One, but the second version may have been painted by Durden as a commission for a recipient in Whitehaven. It is such an accurate duplicate that Durden may have used an original sketch to replicate his work. Exactly when it was painted remains a mystery as well. There was no information on the back of the picture and Durden had left Whitehaven only months later when he enlisted in November of that same year. Did he paint it before he left Moresby or was it done when he returned after the war? By then he was well known enough to be given the commission to design the war memorial on Lowther Street and the Memorial plaque in the church at Moresby. However, the painting remained 'lost' in private hands (possibly with the original recipient) until it was gifted to the Museum in 1982.

61

The Hun's dastardly deeds

THE SHELLING of Lowca by a German submarine during the First World War, highlighted in this column a couple of weeks ago, has unearthed this fascinating postcard commemorating the event.
The postcard was brought in by Mrs Mary Kelly of Earls Road, Bransty, Whitehaven, and appears to have been a propaganda exercise of some kind, declaring, "The latest in German-Hun frightfulness."
From these words I assume the postcard was distributed between the years, 1914-18.
It goes on to say the postcard depicts, "The undefended Cumberland Coast bombarded by Hun Pirates, August 16, 1915", showing where the submarine fired, where some of the shells landed and that the only casualty on that dramatic day was a dog.
In the centre of the photograph can be seen the old flour mills and in the foreground is the Sugar Tongue Pier.

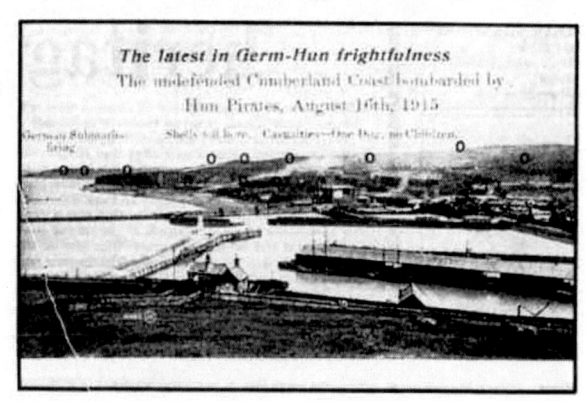

The Bombardment of the Cumberland Coast

On August Sixteenth, old Kaiser Bill
Said to his men, "Now prove your skill,
And try and reach the Cumberland coast,
The feat of which I'd like to boast."

The Kaiser's word they did obey,
And fired away in Parton Bay,
With shot and shell they did their best
To put the Lowca works to rest.

The damage done was not so much,
The Benzol plant they did not touch,
One shell fell here, another there
Which gave the workmen quite a scare.

The inhabitants too grew quite alarmed,
Because this port is still unarmed,
This opportunity the enemy seized,
And rained the shells just where he pleased.

Two shells went through a cottage home,
The father shouts "A German Bomb,"
The children then ran out like bees,
And joined the Lowca refugees.

The submarine then made its way
Across the dub from Parton Bay,
To find some other defenceless port
Where German fiends could have their sport.

8: Private Durden

The attack on the Lowca works indicated that the First World War was now very close to home. Two months later Durden enlisted in the army.

In order to follow Durden through his war, I accessed as many of his military records that I could find. Unfortunately some of these were caught in a fire at some point, so working with charred copies with burnt edges was not the most successful of tasks. Some papers and forms I would really liked to have seen were simply not available and inevitably there are big gaps in his movements.

James enlisted on 30th November, 1915, probably in Whitehaven and he is listed as part of the Special Reserve on 1st December. His occupation is given as 'Artist', though he started his army career as a 'storeman'. On the 23rd May 1916, he is recorded as being 38 years and 6 months old, 5ft 8 inches tall and weighing 129 pounds. His waist measurement is 36 and a half inches and he is described as having a "good pulse". A fragment of his demobilisation paper shows that he became part of the Royal Army Ordnance Corps and he was mobilised on the 29th September 1916.

By the 3rd of October 1916 Durden is in Woolwich. His occupation is still artist and his army service now features the word 'clerk'. He has to provide details of his family and his marriage to Ruby Valentina Ellis is shown as taking place on 30th July 1907 in Surrey. The date and place of birth of children, if any, are also required and Betty and Joseph are duly recorded. Betty was born in Kingston on the 3rd June 1908 and Joseph Valentine in Barnes on the 20th October 1910. This official form

63

Private Durden

was stamped for Private J. Durden on the 3rd November 1916. Interestingly enough Ruby's address on the 24 th November 1916 is shown as "temporarily" at the Central Hotel, Andover, Hants, and she may have travelled down to the south coast to see her husband?

Durden was finally sent abroad on the 3rd April 1917 when he left Folkestone and disembarked at Boulogne. After that the trail goes cold. It looks as if he was in France from the 3rd of April 1917 until the 31st January 1918. One fragment of his Army Documentation, a form headed

'Record of Promotion, Reductions, Transfers, Casualties during Active Service', indicates that he was granted leave on the 1st April 1918 to the 15th April 1918. The Armistice was signed on the 11th November 1918, and he was home for Christmas that year from the 23rd of December to 6th January 1919. One can only imagine the excitement of Ruby and the children at having him back in Orchard House in for the joy of Christmas. This document adds 4th Rate CP to his name on the 1st March 1919 and then transfers him to H6 for 'dispersal'.

The final document fragment is mercifully a lot clearer. It is a Protection Certificate and Certificate of Identity and was plainly James' demobilisation paper releasing him from the army. He was now a soldier not remaining with the colours. This was stamped at Woolwich on the 19th May 1919 and at Prees Heath, Shropshire, on 20th May1919. James was identified as a Private in the R.A.O.C. (the Royal Army Ordnance Corps) with a regimental number of 023528. He signed to say he received an advance of £2 and was granted 28 days furlough. After that uniform will not be worn except upon occasions authorised by Army Orders. His date of birth was recorded incorrectly as 1897 and his medical category was B1. His place of "rejoining in case of emergency" is Heaton Park and he gave his address for pay as Orchard House, Moresby, Whitehaven. His final discharge documents would be sent there too. This is actually an important Certificate as any demobilised soldier or sailor would have to produce it when applying for Unemployed Donation Policy or applying for Unemployment Benefit. It was issued to James

65

War Memorial in Lowther Park, Whitehaven

Durden and if it fell into the possession of any unlawful person they are liable to a fine of £20 or imprisonment for 6 months or both.

James Durden served 304 days and for this he was awarded the regular medals recognising his service to his King and Country participating in 'The Great War for Civilisation 1914 - 1919' (as quoted one medal).

He was also awarded a silver medal for his service at Zeneghem in 1918. The reverse of this medal shows a crest design of 3 heavy artillery guns and the words Army Ordnance Corps. Zeneghem wharf is on the Aa river near the junction of the Calais canal. When the first quay was completed in October 1916, gunes, ammunition and artillery produced in England was shipped to either Dunkirk or Calais and then loaded onto barges to Zeneghem and then deployed by rail to wherever they were needed on the Western Front. It was a massive logistical exercise. At one stage 3000 tons of ammunition were being uploaded daily. Durden, as either a storeman or clerk would be supporting the administrative work demanded by the collation and transport of such ammunition. .

On a lighter side, we do know that Durden was involved in keeping the social side of army life thriving. A programme, from 1918, for 'Grand Xmas Pantomime of Aladdin and his Lamp . . A Pantomime in Two Acts and Eight Gas Attacks' states that "the whole of the scenery was painted by Pte. Durden".

The War Memorial in the Castle Park Gardens on Lowther Street in Whitehaven was designed by James Durden R A and made by Thomas Preston. It sits in the attractive and peaceful park and is the first impressive and dramatic feature you see as you enter the main gate. The 3 step plinth gives way to the column headed with the words "To Our Glorious Dead". The lowest step incorporates a plaque added at a later date commemorating those who gave their lives in the war of 1939 - 1945. No names are listed for either conflict.

The front face of the column is decorated with a relief figure representing Victory and is the traditionally personified lady in classic dress draped in folds. She is holding a laurel wreath in her hands. Durden created the conventional figure which was the accepted form for many of the war memorials the length and breadth of the country to celebrate Victory. They are a product of their age and Durden has obviously fulfilled his brief whilst creating the sort of lady dressed in beautiful drapes who could easily have featured in one of the swathed fashions of his paintings of Betty in the future. The other 3 sides of the column are plain.

In the Autumn sunshine when Dave and I were there, the park with its rather dusty grass and last nod in the direction of a summer gone, seemed a whole world away from the experiences of James and his compatriots. It stands as a permanent memorial to everything that James and his fellows did during those years between 1914 and 1919.

Memorial plaque in Moresby Church

9: Millbeck

In 1914 as the world was about to be engulfed by 'a war to end all wars', a single lady called Grace Tollemache was living peacefully in a beautiful house in the Lake District. She wrote a poem whilst in residence called *The Everlasting Hills.*

Grace Tollemache was a titled lady as well as a poet. She was the daughter of Wilbraham Frederick, Lord Tollemache of Helmingham Hall and Mary Stuart who was born in Holyrood Palace in Scotland. Grace was born in 1869 and her father was a member of Parliament. She was an only child and was brought up surrounded by an impressive household containing a governess, a housekeeper, lady's maid, a cook, housemaids, kitchen maids, a butler and a footman. She was still at home in 1891, but possibly either abroad or travelling in 1901. However by 1911 she was living completely on her own in 24, Hanover Court, Hanover Square. There were no servants and she was recorded as aged 42, single and living on *independent means.*

There is no record of how or why she made the rather surprising move to the Lake District. She purchased a house in Underskiddaw near Keswick in 1914 and settled down to pursue her life and work as a poet. She must have been quite a perceptive lady as she foresaw the wider implications of a future conflict which she suspected would definitely not be over by Christmas or even any time soon after that. She expressed her anxiety in the first verse of her poem 'The Everlasting Hills':

> *I was among you, quiet Hills*
> *When like a swiftly-mounting flood,*
> *War rose, and - colder than your rills -*
> *A current ran along my blood*

As the war progressed she was horrified about the chaos and destruction inflicted on France and laments:
> *Old Rheims cathedral all defaced*
> *And rent with shells and Louvain brought*
> *To ashes .....*

However like many people she turns to the hills for support and consolation finding solace in their peace and permanence
> *From ages gone, for ages more.*

The last verse specifically expresses the comfort she finds in the hills surrounding her home:
> *Unbowed, serene, above assault*
> *And over their fraternal heights*
> *As over yours in Heaven's clear vault*
> *The stars at eve will light their lights.*

The poem ends on this encouraging note. *'The Everlasting Hills'* was published in her book *Poems and Sonnets* in 1916.

The house she purchased in the little village of Millbeck was a grand double fronted Georgian residence set on a slight rise above the farms and fields of a really beautiful pastoral valley with views showing Derwentwater and stretching towards the jaws of Borrowdale and the higher fells beyond. It was called Skiddaw Bank and the spectacular Skiddaw range of mountains rose behind the house. Originally it was the property of Daniel Dover, initially a partner, but then the owner of the thriving woollen industry situated in Underskiddaw in the mid 19th century. Daniel and his son Arthur significantly extended the house in Victorian times, but by the end of the century the woollen industry had died and the remains of both property and land were sold off. Arthur had no offspring and the house passed to Emily Banks and then Ernest Banks who sold it to the Hon Grace Tollemarche in 1914.

In the meantime the Durden family was still in the south of England. The 1911 Census records them living at 36, Madras Road, Barnes with Betty, two years old and Joseph, five months old. There is also a visitor in residence at this point, Jane Elizabeth Mitchell, aged 32. Initially I wondered if this might be a nanny to help Ruby as Janet recalls Betty talking of being looked after by 'Russian Nanny' but this latter lady does not fit the definition and is stated clearly as a visitor. (The Russian Nanny doesn't appear on any census returns). Ruby's parents are still at The Manor House, Beaconsfield Road, Claygate, Surrey.

Interestingly Ruby received a postcard that summer of 1911 indicating that she must have been in St Bees. It was from her sister Lillian (Lily) and was addressed to 1, Victoria Terrace, St Bees, so it looks as if Ruby may have been visiting friends or simply on holiday. Victoria Terrace is quite close to the beach and the whole area was a popular seaside resort.

Whatever the situation we know they are definitely living at Orchard House in Moresby, by the beginning of the war. James comes home after his service and they settle in the Moresby house where James is becoming increasingly successful as an illustrator and an artist.

Ruby's father, Joseph Ellis become a partner in the Lowca works in 1908 purchasing it with Sir John Randle and William Burnyeat. Sometime between 1918 and 1925 the Ellis family moved into Skiddaw Lodge the magnificent Art Deco house next door to Bristowe Hill, the home of Sir John Randles, in Keswick. This house had been purchased by Sir John in 1918 after the death of Leicester Collier, the wealthy art entrepreneur, in 1917. It seems likely that Sir John rented the house out to his business partner and friend, Joseph Ellis.

Certainly the family must have been in residence by February 20th 1925, as the oldest date on the Ellis / Durden gravestones in Crosthwaite Churchyard in Keswick reads, "*In Loving Memory of Sarah Martha Ellis, Beloved wife of Joseph Ellis / Born November 1st 1851……. Died February 20th 1925.* If the matriarch of the Ellis family is laid to rest in Crosthwaite

> **COUNTRY HOUSES AND ESTATES FOR SALE**
>
> **CUMBERLAND**
> Keswick 2 miles, M6 17 miles
>
> In the heart of the National Park enjoying a secluded position with superb views of Derwent Water and surrounding Hills. Listed Period House with 3 Reception rooms, Kitchen, Utility room, 5 Bedrooms, Bathroom. Outbuildings plus 2 Acres. Offers over £25,000. Ref.: 7811.
>
> For further details apply :
> JACKSON-STOPS & STAFF
> 25 Nicholas Street, Chester
> (Tel.: 28361/4)

Guardian June 17th

she probably died whilst the family were in residence at Skiddaw Lodge. (Other names are added to these gravestones when her husband Joseph dies on February 7th 1940, and daughter-in-law Margaret, the wife of Wilfrid in 1958 and son Wilfrid in 1972).

By 1924 Ruby Durden has her elderly parents living in Keswick. Her mother is 73 (and possibly ailing) and her father is 74, so she presumably has to take on the responsibility of whatever care they may or may not need. Geographically, it looks as if she is the nearest relative,.

However in the Spring of 1924 the situation for the Durden family changed again when Grace Tollemache put Skiddaw Bank on the market. It's interesting to speculate why she gave up living in the house, but maybe it became just too isolated and remote and perhaps she found it difficult to settle into a farming community. By now she is 55 and I would guess she will always be regarded with a sort of taciturn respect as an offcomer, a poet and a grand lady with a title. There is no record of whether she joined in the activities at the 1896 Reading Room which developed into a central community hub eventually known as the Village Hall and renowned for its dances and Parish teas! Whatever the reason she returned to London and died 10 years later in January 1934.

So Skiddaw Bank is for sale and here Ruby Durden makes the move that will give James Durden the perfect situation for his artistic gifts and a much loved family home for the rest of his life. The sale documents of Tollemarche to Durden specify the financial details; (involving rentals due for some fields) and are handled by Broatch and Son, Solicitors of Court Buildings

Keswick. The final sale letter dated 6th August 1924 went to Ruby Durden at Broom Villa, Broom House Road, Hurlingham, London indicating that the family still have a property in London. Mr Broatch's last paragraph reads: *Please post the cheque early as letters to the north are sometimes not delivered till late in the afternoon, when it would be too late to arrange with my bankers to pay it over in exchange for the deeds.*

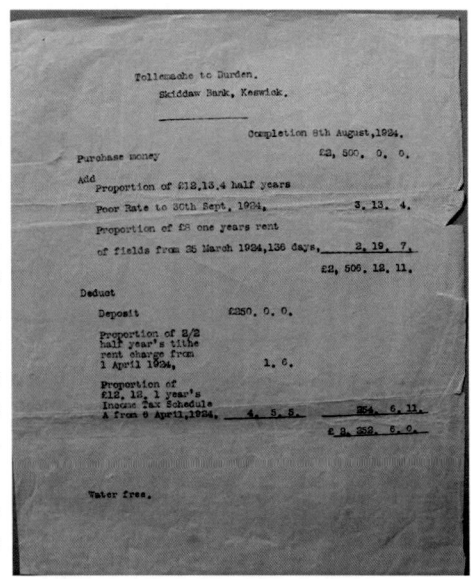

Obviously Ruby complied promptly with this request as the completion document is dated 8th August, 1924, making Ruby Durden the owner of Skiddaw Bank at a cost of £2,500. This becomes the family home for the rest of James and Ruby's lives, although later they also have the Ladbroke Square property in London and Durden is able to divide his time between the capital and the Lake District.

By 1924 the woolen industry in Underskiddaw had declined. The mill buildings around Millbeck Ghyll had been sold or demolished. The Durdens would find themselves living next door to the impressive Millbeck Towers. This was the old carding mill that in 1903 John Banks turned into a residence. Initially he had plans for a Swiss chalet-type house with outside wooden balconies and overhanging windows. However the walls of the old mill were so thick the original window openings had to be retained and he was forced to abandon his scheme. Instead, the front corners of the building were replaced by two pepperpot turrets with large extra windows installed. Inside the old steep steps with accompanying hand ropes were replaced by proper staircases and extra rooms created. The original Mill Bell was preserved and can still be seen outside the building. When the Durdens moved into Skiddaw Bank their neighbours would have been John Banks and family. The property was later occupied by

73

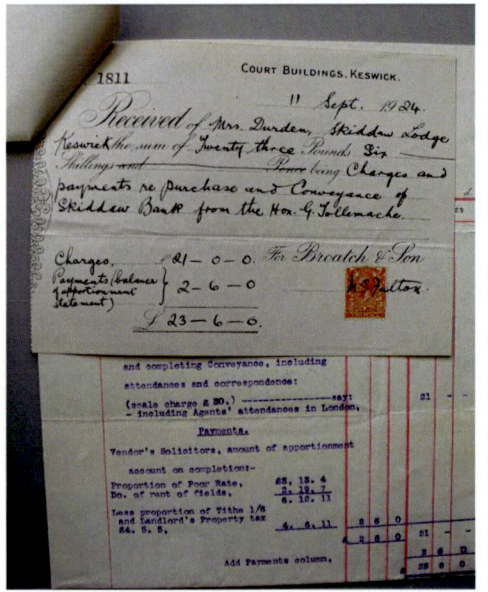

Cecil William Kaye (1865-1941) who was Headmaster of St Bees School from 1917 to 1926. It then passed to his son the inimitable Brigadier James William Kaye R.A. who was commissioned in 1918 and retired in 1949. He bequeathed the house to the National Trust after he died in 1989. The Notes on the History of the Parish of Underskiddaw produced by Grace Fletcher in February 1957 refer to *Skiddaw Bank just above the Mill* (now called Millbeck Place) *and the residence of Mr Durden the artist.* It would appear that the name of the house had changed by this date and this must have been the choice of the Durden family.

Underskiddaw played a significant role in the literary world, with the development of the Romantic Movement during the late 18th and early 19th Century. Southey lived at Greta Hall in Keswick and was briefly joined by Coleridge, who then left his family there. The Wordsworths were in Grasmere. In fact Wordsworth owned a property in Applethwaite at The Ghyll and stories of the literary figures still focused on the village from time to time. The legendary account of the spectacular Bonfire Party on the top of Skiddaw, organised by Southey to celebrate the Waterloo Victory in 1815 must have reached the ears of new occupants of Millbeck Place . The poets were accompanied by visitors and locals and the party got underway with roast beef, plum pudding, rum and punch. The National Anthem was sung around barrels of flaming tar which were rolled down the fell. Wordsworth accidentally knocked over a kettle of boiling water so with no water to dilute it, some of the rum was drunk neat. It must have been a very unsteady torchlit procession back down the fell and apparently one merry maker descended on horseback with face to tail. Skiddaw has always been an accepted location for Bonfire beacons and celebrations and James will probably have heard the stories about his new home over the years.

By the time the Durdens moved into Millbeck Place, the peaceful locality between Applethwaite Ghyll and Millbeck Ghyll consisted of a patchwork of fields and the view from the house showed a number of small farms and attractive old farmhouses dotted around the landscape. These were mostly sheep farms and the farms also included fell grazing areas behind the house on the lower slopes of Skiddaw. The sheep were the white faced Herdwicks, hardy enough to cope with the lake Dustrict weather. Beyond the fields stretched the impressive panorama of the Borrowdale valley flanked by the panorama of fells beyond with Glaramara in sight. The sun when it was evident, rose in the east to the left and sank behind Grisedale Pike to the right. The house was south facing and featured a small terrace to the front. Tea on the terrace became a popular part of the Durden day and James painted the view from that terrace on various occasions and during different seasons. Below the house the quiet terrace road ran along the length of the village and was acknowledged locally as Robert Southey's favourite walk .

Within these pastoral surroundings it is quite understandable that James' artistic career really developed. At some point he converted the coach house and stables at the side of the house to a studio and there he was able to work in peace. Presumably the beautiful drawing room, dining room and generously proportioned kitchen down the three steps at the back of the house were kept free of easels and paint brushes.

Durden paintings were exhibited further afield and in 1927 he was awarded a Medal by the Societe des Artistes, Francais. The prestigious medal features the words *Peinture, Salon de 1927, Durden James*. Durden travelled to Paris to visit the Salon and his reputation within the artistic world was growing. The medal painting was a family portrait. It features Joe seated at one end of a long polished table, Ruby is seated at the opposite end in an armchair and Betty on a dining chair (I have looked at this painting in more detail in the chapter on Portraits and People.) One wonders how he felt about returning to France after his

75

earlier experiences in that country! Janet thinks that the Durdens travelled to Italy in the late 1920's and early 1930's as there are many Italian themed paintings from around this period and they were painted as a result of visits to that country.

Beside landscape painting Durden was now also beginning to reflect the spirit of the new post war age. By now the so-called 'roaring twenties' were well under way. In the aftermath of the war everything in the world of fashion and style changed, particularly for the young, wealthy and elite classes from hair-styles to hem lengths. The popularity of Jazz, motorcars and the freedom to travel created a new world.

Durden's name featured in the prestigious modern magazine called *The Studio ...A magazine of Fine and Applied Art.* In Volume 90, Number 392 published on November 14th, 1925 Durden had five pictures. One was a full page colour plate called *The Green Sun-blind* featuring a lady in a blue dress posed against the sun-blind. Another full length plate in black and white was a portrait of the famous model Irene Dineley and I have examined this painting in more detail in the Portraits chapter. Miss Dineley is the model in the black and white reproduction of a more well known painting called *Black and Gold.* Another full lenght plate is entitled *The Blue Settee* and again is a portrait of an unknown lady, this time reclining on an ornamental brocaded settee. The last painting is smaller and reproduced part way through the article. No figures appear by the simple chair and half moon desk situated by a window at twilight. The curtains aren't yet drawn and the familiar mountain silhouette on the horizon suggests a Millbeck Place setting. Fittingly it is called *Twilight in Cumberland.*

The Studio article was written by Jessica Walker Stephens. She started her analysis by describing Durden's paintings as : *Strong and highly satisfactory examples of the work of the objectivist-decorative school whose hold on. British artists has lasted so long and which has been so little challenged.*

She proceeds to give quite a lengthy analysis of this style and acknowledges Durden's Manchester background. Her last paragraph reads: *His present painting shows some traces of his study of magazine and book illustration, in which he was for some time engaged. His feminine types are dainty and very modern, and he delights in elegance and sophistication, and the beauty pertaining thereto. Mr Durden's chief trait in common with other Manchester born artists is his adherence to light, clean colour and other qualities foreign to Lancashire. He misses no opportunity of painting sunshine seen through windows with all its reflections and values, and he loves the flash of light on glass and polished wood.The work shows a delicate sense of selection and of spacing and brings the restfulness belonging to the exercise of this sense.*

The iconic painting of these early years in Millbeck is of course *Summer in Cumberland* and this beautiful tranquil picture features all that was dear to the artist. The family are shown taking afternoon tea by the open window of the drawing room at Millbeck Place on a glorious afternoon in high summer. In the foreground the elegant Ruby, in her fashionable black dress and pearls bends slightly from her seated position to speak to the attentive and rather fine (but unnamed) black and white cat, who looks to be a much loved member of the family. There is almost the suggestion of feline interest in the oval silver lidded dish on the circular padded stool positioned between the cat and Ruby. One could guess it contained warm muffins or buttered scones. Betty is facing her mother at a slight angle and is settled on the generous full length window seat and in the act of sipping her tea from a delicate China cup and saucer. She appears to have lifted it from the oval tray with silver teapot and accompaniments on the circular table in front of her . She cuts a beautiful youthful figure clad in a light diaphanous summer dress in pastel shades of white pink and grey. Her legs are elegantly crossed and she is wearing a fashionable pair of pale-pink ballet type shoes. The magnificent arched shaped window behind her is open and outside her brother Joseph appears to be waiting. He is only partially shown, but is in whites and gives every impression of waiting to start or finish a game of tennis on the court below in the garden. Maybe he has been called to participate in the tea. On one end of the window seat is a circular pleated cushion and at the other end of the window there is a table with a magnificent classical vase of delphiniums and lupins. The scene is dominated by the spectacular arched window with its view of the valley, the lake and the Derwent Fells in varying shades of blue beyond. The whole scene is illuminated by the sunshine that streams through the window. A little outside foliage in the top left hand corner of the casement casts light and some shadow on this delightful afternoon tea. It captures the spirit of a seemingly endless summer afternoon suffused with golden light and warmth and shows the Durden family each relaxing in these gentle and peaceful surroundings,

It was always assumed that this painting was reproduced exactly as a family picture of afternoon tea and tennis looking from the window of Millbeck Place. Certainly the view from the window on the left hand side of the front door is accurate with the fields, lake and fells beyond. It is possible to identify Castle Crag behind the athletic Joseph's head with the view of Glaramara filling the open window casement in the far distance . However on closer examination the window is not the window of Millbeck Place. This is a bay window the proportions of which extend elegantly at the front of the house. It is matched on the other side of the front door (the dining room), giving the house its balanced two wings. However the windows are simple casements with the middle window consisting of 16 rectangular panes of glass and no arched fan-shaped panel above.

Plainly this is not the window featured in the painting. The magnificent dominant sweep of the arched window used effectively to frame the view is missing and indeed the picture would lose much of its artistic integrity if it featured the rectangular shaped window of the house. So it becomes obvious that James has employed a certain degree of artistic licence here and either created or copied a different window to imaginatively install in his view. One theory is that James used the window as seen and then 'borrowed' the fan-light window above the front door. However various local explanations have different ideas and these arise from the proximity of the Ellis family home.

As we know Ruby's parents were still living on Vicarage

Summer in Cumberland
Manchester City Gallery

Hill in the stunning Art Deco Skiddaw Lodge. A dark brown wooden staircase in this house is flooded by light from a half landing window probably described originally as a mid vestibule level window. The window is strikingly similar to the one in the 'Summer in Cumberland' painting. It contains the same smaller panels of glass and is crowned by a superb fan window, showing the same arrangement of panes as the one in the painting. James must have been a frequent visitor to his parents-in-law and it seems likely that this window attracted his attention. It's quite possible that he decided to use it to enhance the rather plainer window in Skiddaw Bank in his painting thus adding height to the window and using it to frame the view beyond. This theory has since been supported by Janet Durden Hey, the artist's grand-daughter who has always maintained that the window in the picture was not the one in Millbeck Place . She remembers the Skiddaw Lodge feature as the likely model taken by Durden for his painting, as does Peter Nelson another local artist familiar with the Durden collection.

Whatever the provenance, the painting had an instant freshness and appeal and was sold within 12 months. One has to congratulate Manchester Art Gallery on their purchase in 1926 and it still features in their collection. It has made various appearances over the years and always excited critics, academics and viewers.

In 1985 the Victoria and Albert Museum featured the picture on the cover of a promotional brochure. It was also used as a catalogue cover for an Exhibition *The Discovery of the Lake District: A Northern Arcadia and its Uses.* Durden's family summer painting joined those of Turner and Constable. It was of course, quite different in style and content. The earlier artists showed the ideas of the early intrepid Victorian adventurers exploring the magnificent lands, lakes and mountains of the north. Durdens picture had a more popular modern personal perspective emphasising the joys of a relaxing family experience in beautiful surroundings.

The painting was used again in 2004 when Manchester Metropolitan University used it in an exhibition at Manchester Art Gallery as part of a selection of paintings considered as therapeutic. The project became a 'Tranquillity Tour' for visitors and featured *Thompson's Aeolian Harp* by Turner, and *Autumn Leaves* by Millais. Interesting research showed a reduction in stress levels amongst participants taking the tour with Durden's picture being highlighted as the painting that caused visitors to stand and apparently relax, stopping for a longer time in front of

Sitting room with Blue Sofa at Millbeck

it than they did when viewing other pictures.

Durden went on to paint other views from Millbeck Place at all times of year. It's obviously a view the artist enjoyed. There is a lovely picture of the view from the terrace in the snow and an attractive presentation of the same place with its sun umbrella and the pink rhododendron in full bloom, I have analysed some of these in the chapter called A Sense of Place.

On a cold and rather dull morning in February 2022 my husband and I went to Manchester Art Gallery to see 'Summer in Cumberland'. It was a major part of their impressive Exhibition about the Tea and Coffee Trade and I was so thrilled to see the original picture. It has of course been perfectly

Sunny dining room - Millbeck 1927

preserved by the Gallery and I was immediately struck by the vibrancy of the colours. It was very obvious that the print on my living room wall did not do justice to the original beautiful work of art. The familiar colours suddenly had a major impact and I was particularly excited about the range of the blue shades which seemed unexpectedly far more noticeable than previously. The vase of delphiniums on the print had always seemed peripheral, but now the fresh cobalt blue of the flowers made their own impact as did hazy purple/grey blues of fells and sky. Even the contrasting black and white of the cat seemed so much more realistic and very clear. Of course the major impact of the painting comes from the striking effect of glowing sunshine diffusing through the whole scene and the original showed the impressive influence of this golden colour. Light, shadow and reflection appeared in vivid shades and even the ochre yellow of the window seat cover seemed to be highlighted in a way I'd never noticed before. It's a magnificent painting and in my opinion presents James Durden at his best.

I was also delighted to meet the The Fine Arts Curator, Hannah Williamson. She generously took me down to the their Art store to see the painting of the Brown family featured in the chapter on People and Portraits. I was most grateful for the time she spent with me and our subsequent discussion on Durden. Like most Museums and Art Galleries, Manchester possesses little biographical material on Durden and she was pleased to receive the research I had undertaken so far establishing details about the life and work of the artist.

June

Betty and Chu c.1928
Keswick Museum and Art Gallery

10: Betty

Betty Durden, James's only daughter, was born in Kingston in London on June 3rd 1908 and died in Cheshire in 1999. She married fellow artist, Australian Leonard Green, on the 25th October 1933 in Cape Town, South Africa. She was a fascinating, talented and complex character who filled the very different roles of model, daughter and wife. Although seemingly rather quiet and unassuming, she possessed an engaging and strong personality with an entertaining sense of humour and a readiness to take on new challenges. Above all she was a survivor, who weathered life's crises with a resilience which belied her rather small and fragile appearance. Artistically talented, she was modest about her own abilities, preferring to promote her husband's work rather than her own. She held steadfastly to her own beliefs and principles as a naturopath. She was once bitten by a red-backed spider in Australia and refused conventional medication. This was a risky strategy, but she survived it all unscathed.

By the time Betty was 18, the era known as 'The Roaring Twenties' was well under way. The First World War had ended and peace brought huge socio-economic change and a real sense of optimism to a post-war world. However, it was a decade of massive contrast. Some had prospered, such as the manufacturers and suppliers of goods needed for the war effort and they benefited from the huge profits. The 'bright young things' from the aristocracy and wealthy classes proceeded to enjoy life to the full, taking advantage of new freedoms and new opportunities. Travel and the advent of the motor car opened up new horizons. Unchaperoned trips were suddenly acceptable. New exciting musical trends from the Jazz age in America arrived bringing the hugely popular Charlston dance. Jazz clubs and cocktail bars flourished.

Women from most classes benefited from new freedoms. During the war many had been employed in factories and a wage had given them a new sense of independence. Women over 30 were given the vote in 1918 and by 1928 this had been extended to women over 21. All this manifested itself in a new sense of confidence and empowerment. Children benefited too with the 1921 Education Act raising the new school leaving age to 14 and state primary education became free for all children.

At 21, Betty did not go to a finishing school as was the custom for her social class, but spent time with her brother Joe at his school, Alpine College in Switzerland where she learned to ski. In the meantime Durden continued to use his daughter as his model and his pictures of her reflected the spirit of the age. There is no evidence to suggest that Betty ever became a socialite flapper, but she certainly looked the part in some of the paintings. Fashion became an integral part of this new age with modernisation as the key factor. Dresses showed shorter hemlines and dropped waistlines. They were loosely cut concealing rather than defining the figure and encouraging a flat chested almost boyish look. Simple lines with minimal adornment arrived, but expensive fabrics such as silk, velvet and satin were used. Evening dresses were low cut supported only by shoulder straps and this revealed far more of the arms and legs than ever before. Gone was the corset, buttons and lacing to be replaced by metal hooks and eyes, zips and press studs to fasten clothing. In fact the term 'flappers' was the popular name given to these fashionable young ladies because of the loose clothes they wore. Almost inevitably hairstyles also changed and hair was neatly coiled or cut short in a new bob. It was conveniently tucked under a small hat or cloche to complete the look .

With his impressive sense of colour and texture James must have been delighted to go along with these new fashionable fabrics and fashions and pose his beautiful daughter in such modes. She was the perfect model for him and looked wonderful

Betty on the Balcony

in the strapped evening dress or modern outfits. The new extravagant fabrics gave Durden the opportunity to depict flowing dresses with folds and drapes artistically arranged on a standing or seated Betty. Fabrics again were featured in backgrounds with the suggestion of cascading curtains, sometimes with further patterns. Often an occasional accessory, such as a small table with a vase of flowers (cobalt blue delphiniums), or bowl of fruit (oranges) was used and always in vibrant colours.

One of my favourite paintings is called Betty and Chou, part of the collection bequeathed by Durden to Keswick Museum and Art Gallery. It's a glazed oil on canvas and shows Betty seated on a low long stool with a curtained background and the family dog at her feet. She is wearing a short evening dress in a silver grey fabric with the folds catching the light. It is a simple strap design revealing the neck, shoulders and arms. One hand rests casually in her lap with the other out of sight behind her angled legs. The stool is covered with similar silvery grey material. The figure of Betty contrasts vividly with the sweeping fabric behind her. It is a vibrant turquoise colour and is decorated with a golden pattern to one side of Betty, depicting an exotic bird of prey in partial flight with one extended wing. The wing is almost suggestive of a peacock tail with tiered feathers in blues, reds, pinks and creams. The pattern is complemented by a smaller similar bird at rest further down the fabric and some brief suggestions of a tree and some random leaves. The colours produce a striking and dramatic contrast and it makes for a spectacular portrait.

Rather unusually in the left hand corner of this painting we have the other eponymous occupant of the title. This is Chou, also perfectly posed and demonstrating an impressive example of the 'sit and stay' school of doggy obedience. Chou or Chu is an Akita breed of dog and looks quite young with rather a fluffy coat and a most attractive face. Initially I wondered if he might be a borrowed accessory, but given that he features on a family holiday photograph this appears not to be the case. He is shown on the photographs of the caravan holiday in Cornwall in 1933 sitting at Ruby's feet. Akitas are Japanese mountain dogs bred for hunting across difficult terrain. Consequently they are large, powerful, broad chested animals and can be quite difficult to control. On the credit side they are loyal and affectionate with one family and also very territorial. They are intelligent and make excellent watch dogs. The Japanese describe them as 'tender in heart and strong in strength.' They are rather noble and dignified looking dogs. Judging by Chu's appearance on this painting, he appears to be meeting all the characteristics of the breed. He looks perfectly relaxed and happy to sit where he has been placed. There is another painting of him in a portrait called 'A woman with a book sitting by a window'.

In October 1933 the dynamic between father and daughter must have changed as Leonard Green moved permanently into both Betty's life and the Durden family. Leonard Green, known as Leon (pronounced Len) was born in Menzies, Western Australia on the 12th February 1905. His parents were Patrick James Green and Agnes Bridget Fleming. On his flying certificate from London Air Park Flying School in 1937 his nationality is given as British in spite of being born in Australia. His profession is given as 'Artist'. The London Air Park Flying School also known as Hanworth Air Park was located on the South-East edge of Feltham in the grounds of Hanworth Park House. It was a known for the manufacture of aircraft. In November 1928 the National Flying Services was formed as a central organisation to co-ordinate a national network of aerodromes and flying clubs. It was renamed as London Air Park, based at Hanworth House and opened by the Duchess of Bedford on August 31st 1929. The first training aircraft were Simonds Spartans de Havilland 60 X Moths and de Havilland 60 M Moths (which match the details on Leon's certificate). During the 1930's the School became a popular centre for society events such as Garden Party fly-ins (aerial tea parties), air pageants and air races. It was visited by a Graf Zeppelin airship and several V.I.P's including Stanley Baldwin, Louis Bleriot, Barbara Cartland, Amy Johnson and various foreign diplomats and royalty. My personal opinion of Leon is very much based on the Durden family dealings, but I'm tempted to think Leon would have loved all this … the excitement of learning to fly this light aircraft, gaining a certificate and being involved in society events. Significantly this certificate is also useful as it indicates that Leon and presumably Betty were back in London in 1937. There is no record of this visit anywhere else in the Archive.

Whether or not Leon was welcomed into the Durden family is debatable. One is tempted to comment on the irony of a situation almost repeating itself. The Ellis family had their reservations about James as a suitable match for Ruby and now it seems that James was doubtful about Leonard Green. This observation is backed by the fact that within the Archive there is a copy of an 'Antenuptial Contract'. It is dated 23rd of October 1933 which is only 2 days before the wedding. This seems rather a last minute event - did the Durdens insist on it being signed and sealed before the ceremony? and did Betty go along with it just to keep her father happy? It was issued by Colin George Cowan Wrentmore of 107, St George's street CapeTown between 'Leonard James Green, a bachelor of full age of 16 Thornhill Flats, Green Point' and 'Betty Durden, a spinster of full age, recently of 4 Ladbroke Square, London W11, now of Cape Town'. Five conditions were specified

1. No community of profit (meaning that all individual assets were to be retained by both parties with no access to them by the other partner)
2. Neither of them should be held liable for any debts incurred by the other
3. All inheritances, gifts or bequests shall be the sole property of him or her
4. Either consort shall be allowed to dispose of their own property without consultation or hindrance from the other

5. This agreement overrides any marital claims on her property or assets.

It becomes clear from these clauses that the Durdens really wished to protect their daughter from any legal claims Leonard might have on Betty's property, possessions or estate. Reading between the lines one could reasonably conclude that James and Ruby didn't really trust their future son-in-law. They could protect their daughter's financial situation if not her happiness!

A special licence was issued for the ceremony which took place at St. Saviours Church, Claremont, Cape Town on 25th October 1933. It was witnessed by James and Ruby. The wedding photograph shows a very happy couple. There appears to be no elaborate wedding dress or several bridesmaids and it doesn't look as if Betty has emulated the weddings of her Ellis cousins back in England. She is wearing an ankle length box pleated dress with long sleeves and white collar and cuffs. The buttoned bodice gives the impression of a jacket but looks as if it is an integral part of the dress. This is accessorised by a small beret-like hat worn at an angle and decorated with three integrated bows as part of the design. The black and white photo in the archive gives no indication of colour, but the white of collar and cuffs show up as a contrast, suggesting that the outfit was a pale colour. It looks as if the ceremony has been concluded, as Betty is clutching rather than formally holding a small bag and some rather creased gloves. If there were any flowers it looks as if they have been put down somewhere. She is absolutely beaming at her new husband in his fashionably smart suit with collar and tie and white handkerchief in the breast pocket. His outfit is completed by a dark coloured homburg hat and the beaming smile is reciprocated. Whatever the concerns of her parents and whatever the future may hold this is undoubtedly a very happy day for the bride and groom.

Prior to the marriage, the Durden family had one last holiday together. The family were about to be involved in the major upheaval of travelling to South Africa for the wedding, where James had arranged an exhibition in Capetown. (When they set sail they were accompanied by a considerable number of James's paintings.)

Before the journey and all the excitement, the family went to Cornwall in August 1933 for a holiday. They owned a caravan which Janet recalls used to stand in the field behind Millbeck Place. It bears the registration plate of the car YH 9886 and is very much a product of its time. It looks very heavy and rather cumbersome, but nevertheless, it was towed from Cumberland to Cornwall that last summer before Betty's departure.

One delightful photograph from that holiday shows a happy family group seated in front of the caravan. The back of the caravan is facing the camera with the upper section of the traditional stable door partially open. The striped curtain is visible and the view through the van to the opposite door reveals the trees or hedge beyond. Parked by the caravan is the car and on the opposite side it's possible to see the tented canvas open awning and groundsheet. It's also possible to make out the outline of a folding table with some sort of globular shaped light hanging above it. The family are relaxing in the foreground of the picture. On the left Betty is seated on a deck chair and appears to be laughing, possibly at some comment of her brother Joe sitting on the caravan running board next to her. We've seen so many paintings of the rather expressionless Betty in flowing gowns that it's a delight to see the real person giggling and relaxed. She is wearing a very ordinary striped dress and cardigan and is rather slumped back in the deck chair with her arms folded in front of her. However the little cloche hat is still in evidence and the popular double t-bar shoes. Joe, in an open necked white shirt, but still in a suit, is also smiling broadly and displays the dark haired good looks seen in previous pictures. Ruby, looking rather older now, is wearing glasses and is holding firmly onto the beautiful Chu (Chou). He dominates the central area of the photograph and is clearly very interested in something off camera towards his left. Sharing this top step of the running board with Ruby is a small fair-haired boy with a deep wickerwork basket in his hands. He is snuggled up quite close to Ruby, but this may simply be because of lack of space on the seat. There is no clue about the identity of this child and it's possible that he is simply a little lad delivering eggs from a nearby farm. Finally we have James completing the group sitting in a folding camping chair. He too is in an open-necked white shirt, but in a jumper with the sleeves rolled up and lighter more casual looking trousers. He is neither smiling or facing the camera and frankly he looks a little pre-occupied and tired. Maybe he is recovering from the monumental task of towing that caravan from Millbeck to Cornwall! It's an absolutely delightful photograph and truly records the closing stages of the

Durden family as such. I love it!

There is another photograph from that holiday worthy of note. It shows Betty standing on a rock with every appearance of being on her way down to a beach. The vest top and shorts could well constitute a swimsuit and she is almost in mid stride looking as if she is about to step onto the sand. The Durdens must have been lucky that August of 1933, with enough sunshine to enjoy the delights of the Cornish coast and each other's exclusive company for the last time.

Everything changes the following month when the ship called the Carnarvon Castle sails from Southampton to Capetown on the 29th September. On the passenger list is the Durden family, James, 55 and an artist, Ruby a housewife, Betty (no further designation) and Joseph aged 22 described as a biologist. The family stay in South Africa for 6 months and the passenger lists for 12th March 1934 show the return of James Durden 56, of 4 Ladbroke Square, London, artist and wife Ruby also 56, housewife and Joseph but with no defined occupation this time.

In the meantime the Exhibition of Paintings by J. Durden R.O.I. eventually went ahead at Ashley's Galleries on Church Street in CapeTown from February 5th to 10th,1934. It received rather mixed reviews and I have devoted part of the chapter called 'Fame' to this and subsequent events and exhibitions.

It is not known how long Betty and Leon stayed in South Africa (or even quite what they were doing there). Leonard was an artist, but there is little evidence that this occupation supported their lifestyle. They both really enjoyed the outdoor life. They both loved ski-ing and at some point Leon was an enthusiastic ski instructor. Whatever they were doing in South Africa they were back in London three years later when Leon developed another interest and skill and took up flying.

Betty and Leon remained in London between 1937 and the beginning of World War 2. They spent time with Joe who by now had met his future wife, Kathleen Iris Meredith. She was living in the flat above the Ladbroke Square accommodation occcupied by James and Ruby. Joe and Kathleen married in 1938. Joe had an interesting story of blocking the wireless reception whenever

Leon wanted to listen to Lord Haw-Haw's propaganda broadcasts from Germany.

Leon decided that he would prefer to be back in his native Australia at this point and he and Betty left London and spent most of the 1940's there. They were able to indulge their love of the outdoors with some interesting accounts from Betty of their adventures. They did quite a lot of travelling in the Outback, trekking and camping. Extended painting trips took place and skiing trips were high on the agenda. The accepted earlier paintings of the model Betty by her father couldn't be more in contrast to the pictures of Mrs Green that emerged during these years in Australia. Leon was from a farming background and Betty developed a new and impressive set of skills. One photo shows her milking a cow. Her sleeves are rolled up and her shirt tucked into some serviceable slacks, with her feet pushed into some flat toeless sandals. She looks strong, confident and competent. How's that as a change from standing on a balcony wearing a diaphanous silver flowing gown? There is also a photo of her on horseback, although she doesn't look quite as confident and the outfit of skirt, blouse and cardigan doesn't really seem to fit the bill. It rather looks as if she is riding sidesaddle. There is another striking photograph of Betty and Leon on a ski-ing holiday.

So during World War ll, Betty and Leon appeared to settle for good in Australia. James and Ruby retreated to the comparative peace of Millbeck .However it would appear that the Green marriage went through a difficult phase and they separated for a period. Janet says nothing further was said and although problems were alluded to, no discussion ever followed. However in February 1949 a letter from Betty to her parents shows that she was back in London and some suggestion of a reconciliation with Leon was suggested. I have quoted from this letter towards the end of this chapter.

Certainly by 1950 the restless Leon reappeared and the couple reunited. They went off to the continent on a skiing trip and by 1958 were settled together again, this time living in Hampstead. Sketching expeditions and more skiing trips followed. There were always the finances to consider and the couple made quite an issue of finding the cheapest way to travel and fund their life style. They were also also spending time in Millbeck where the situation with Betty's parents took a crisis turn when Ruby became ill.

Betty returned to the house to look after James and Ruby, but Ruby died on 21st April 1958. A devastated James needed company and possibly some care, so Betty and Leon came to live with him.

This was not the right decision for Leon. One can only imagine what this artist made of the Cumbrian climate with its poor light in the winter and the possibility of mist and torrential rain all year round. This is a man who has been brought up in Australia and lived in South Africa and loves skiing in Europe. Millbeck in February must have been an absolute joy! Added to that Millbeck Place was now really showing its age and maintenance was becoming expensive and never ending. As soon as one aspect of the building was fixed something else went wrong and the struggle to stay on top of it all seemed to have mainly devolved on the unfortunate Leon. He longed for their old life of travel and adventure and very definitely a warmer climate. His frustration was somewhat alleviated by occasional trips for skiing and painting to Spain and Austria, but neither he or Betty ever really settled back in Cumberland.

They, or rather Betty, soldiered on and it must have been a comfort to James to have his daughter back under his (occasionally leaking) roof. They were visited by Joe and Kathkeen's daughter Janet in 1960 and having a bright and talented 16 year old around until 1961 must have been a like breath of fresh air! This was followed by an expedition in 1963 as James and Betty travelled to Boston in America to see Joe and Kathleen who had emigrated to Canada in 1952. Seeing his son again must have been a real pleasure for the aging widower. He was extremely proud of this gifted son who had come to prominence in the scientific circles of Boston and developed the name and reputation of the world's leading cine -biologist.

It was to be James's last trip away from Millbeck and during the following winter his health deteriorated significantly. Betty continued to care for him until he was admitted to the Cottage Hospital in Keswick, where he died on November 9th, 1964. He was 86 and it is all credit to Betty that she cared for him, devotedly during the closing stages of his life. It must have been a real comfort to him to have his much loved only daughter by his side when he needed her most .

So Betty, and by default Leon, inherited Millbeck Place and they continued to live there after James's death. The problems didn't go away and the whole situation just exacerbated Leon's increasing disillusionment with most aspects of his life. Something had to change, so it was decided to utilise the barn belonging to Millbeck Place, which James had used as a studio. Surely it would be possible to convert part of this barn into simpler accommodation which would be easier to manage and more or less maintenance free. Leon was keen on the idea of also incorporating a section of the barn into a Gallery to showcase various works (more of his own than his father in law's). The decision was made and in 1972 Millbeck Place was sold to two retired doctors and their family. (The Tyson family loved the property and location and it was only sold after the death of widow, Dr Peggy Tyson). Betty and Leon went ahead with the planned conversion and moved into their new home and Art Gallery now next door to Millbeck Place.

Although the problems of maintaining Millbeck Place had been handed on to the Tysons, nothing else had been solved for the restless Leon. His high hopes of running a Gallery soon diminished. The new gallery was too remote to attract anyone, let alone the intelligentsia or critics of the Art world. It soon became apparent that combining a studio, Art Gallery and living accommodation wasn't the solution Leon anticipated and there was always the unpredictable weather! In spite of a few trips away, by 1980 Leon had developed yet another dream. All would be well if they went back to Australia and started a new life there. As always Betty agreed. She always went along with her husband's dreams and time after time genuinely believed in all his enthusiastic new schemes. He was 80 by now and she was 72, but off they went to a brave new world to start again. The Studio Barn was sold to an Artist and local dentist Peter Nelson in 1980 and a new house outside Perth in Australia was purchased. They sailed for Australia taking many Durden paintings and some valuable furniture with them.

Joe and Kathleen Durden visited them in 1981 and found Leon in characteristic enthusiastic mode developing the house and new garden with Betty's support. Leon's family were still in the area and it looked initially as if the relocation would give both Betty and Leon a new and happier lifestyle.

Almost predictably it didn't! In 1988, they (or Leon) decided Australia wasn't working out and they needed to return to England to start a new life! So with yet another blank canvas they looked for a new area. One can almost hear Leon declaring 'anywhere but the Lake District!" but the choice of venue now completely baffled everyone. They bought a bungalow in Milton Keynes. This was apparently because they would be in easy reach of travelling to the continent, especially for skiing holidays, and this was a dream that Leon was definitely not going to abandon. Most of the paintings and furniture that had been shipped out to Australia were now shipped back to Milton Keynes. The spare bedroom and garage filled up with packing cases.

Leon was still very active and in the Spring of 1993 a skiing holiday was booked to Austria. Before the holiday could take place however Leon cut himself on the corner of a packing case in the garage. It's not known how much the naturopath Betty influnced Leon, but no medical intervention occurred and Leon died at home on 24th May 1993. Janet thought that Leon may have died of blood poisoning, but the death certificate records the cause of death as 'Myocardial Infarction' and 'Ischaemic Heart Disease'.

Betty was now left on her own and it quickly became apparent how much Leon had sustained their lifestyle. Money had

Betty Durden (Green): Red rooves landscape

always been in short supply and was usually supplemented by the sale of a painting or piece of furniture. Their finances were unpredictable at the best of times and had always been managed by Leon. Betty really had only a vague under-standing of how their finances functioned. Leon planned everything from holidays to food shopping and cooking, although Betty was very specific about their diet. Although she could drive she had done so less and less and Leon had driven her everywhere in recent times. Mentally she was still very much alert and prepared to accept all life's vicissitudes. Janet described her as having an almost *Buddhist like attitude*'. This was perhaps as well because she was now in a totally unsustainable situation. She had no children to turn to and not even any close friends around her. The situation was deteriorating and could only get worse.

At this point Janet and husband David Hey came to her rescue and helped Betty move from Milton Keynes to Cheshire to be close to her remaining family. She died on 17th Feb.1999 at Sandiway Lodge, Dalefords Lane, Sandiway, Northwich. The death certificate issued on the 19th February records a 'chest infection' as the cause of death. Her ashes were brought up to Keswick, so she could join her beloved husband. Interestingly, the occupation on her death certificate was given as Widow of Leonard James Green, Artist (Retired) and I'm sure she would

Betty Durden (Green): Village green with church 1949

consider this as an accurate description of her life's work.

Janet was able to give me a lot of detail about this talented lady . . . her success as a 'cordon bleu' cook, her ability to make silk flowers and work with Japanese flower arranging. She learned to weave, sew and work with wood. Amusingly Janet remembers Betty teaching her how to eat fruit, when spending Christmas with rather grand friends. She remembers how she couldn't let the side down, but nor could she peel grapes with cutlery.

There is no doubt that Betty was a talented artist in her own right. Within the Durden archive is a large hardbacked black ring folder. It measured 17 x14 inches and was labelled

Betty Durden Green, WATERCOLOURS and SKETCHES.

A letter from Betty to her parents possibly gives a clue as to the origin of this book. It was sent in mid-February 1949 from Rhodesia Court Hotel. Harrington Gardens, Kensington, from a very excited Betty, who had just arrived from Australia. It starts *Pinch me to see if it is really true! It is.* She was delighted to be home and is full of the journey back (with a delay at Port Said) and interested in the way everything has changed in England. *The shops are absolutely wonderful, full of stuff that looks better than prewar and the prices are no more than in Sydney, some much less and the food is half the price. The shops are full of fruit and vegetables . . .*

The main point of this chatty and exuberant letter however is to explain why she has not yet made the journey North.

I am just longing to see you, however I think we shall have to leave it for two or three weeks, normally I should have dashed right up without taking breath, but under the present circumstances I feel I had better take this proposed holiday with Leon, he has suggested it and as we have seen so little of each other in the past three years and have grown so far apart I feel this may be the beginning of better things to come so I am hoping you won't feel hurt at being left a little longer and will understand.

These present circumstances refer to the problem already mentioned with the relationship with Leon and a possible break in the marriage. This proposed trip to Switzerland appears to be important to both of them. Leon is anxious to go before the snow disappears as it gives him a chance to pursue a study on different skiing methods which he wishes to photograph. Betty is full of travel plans and reading between the lines she appears hopeful that this holiday will rescue the flagging marriage.

The other significant point in this letter is concerned with the sketch book and it looks as if this is where it all started . Betty says: *This afternoon we payed (sic) a visit to the Poly where we were welcomed by most of the old staff and Brownswood, who is now head, gave us the run of the place so to speak, we can both go any time we like and do anything we like which is more than decent of them as they are taking on new students. Leon is going to concentrate on anatomy and drawing and I hope to learn a bit more about designing and printing.*

This is exactly what Betty did and the sketch book is an impressive representation of her talents. There is an auxiliary sketch book slipped inside the main file called 'Botanical Studies' which contains 17 pages of practice exercises of various plants and flowers. Some are pencil sketches, some are completed water colours, some are tentative outlines and many are accompanied by the Latin name and detailed pencil notes about the specimen

Betty Durden (Green)
Lake with trees & yachts 1949

and the colours.

The rest of the contents of the black ring folder are equally striking and significant in that they show an impressive range of material. One loose sheet at the beginning is a detailed pencil sketch of the head and shoulders of an elderly gentleman in profile. It's a magnificent portrait with accurate shading and emphasis highlighting the high forehead, receding hair-line and perfectly proportioned ear and an aquiline nose. Betty's initials are in the corner and Janet thinks the gentleman was probably an art class model.

There are some completed paintings of various landscapes and this portfolio is now beginning to look like a submission for the purposes of the course. A whole series of harbour paintings of an unknown location are dated 1949. There are some lovely pictures of unidentified villages, further studies of botanical specimens and some Alpine paintings.

Finally Betty fulfilled her ambition to look at design and printing and the portfolio contains some impressive samples of repeat patterns. My favourite sheet is a series of experimental

Betty Durden (Green): Designs

efforts at presenting domestic fowl. It features two partially completed turkeys and several outlines or completed miniature paintings of cockerels. I really liked them and I think Betty has successfully captured the bobbing movement of a pecking bird and the typical pose of a bird standing on one leg in the top corner of the page.

I hesitate to develop this chapter any further, although the potential for a full art appreciation is obviously screaming for attention. Betty deserves a full book all to herself, but I'm mindful that this little book is more about James Durden and not his talented daughter, so there I will close her sketch book. It was displayed as part of the 2021 Exhibition at Keswick Museum and Art Gallery and much enjoyed by visitors. The fabulous portraits done by her father gave the Exhibition its title of BETTY'S BACK and she became a significant part of the Gallery presentation.

Finally, she was an artist, but living with Leon meant that his efforts were always more important than her own. The letter and sketch book establish that she had some Art School training. She painted in watercolours, rather than oils. Her sense of structure and design and her use of delicate colours is delightful. In some ways her considerably lesser known lovely gentle water colours, often of simple rural landscapes, can easily rival her father's more professional and grand oil paintings.

Betty was a woman of many parts. She was the model for James Durden's portraits, a devoted daughter and wife. However, above all else I think that Betty Green is an artist!

11: The Bridesmaid

In 1927 Durden painted an iconic picture of Betty. He called it *The Bridesmaid*. It's an oil on canvas measuring 181 x 135 cms. and is spectacular both in size and striking appearance. It's now on permanent display in the Exhibition and Art gallery space at Keswick Museum. The arresting figure of the seated Betty and the contrasting and dominant colours in the painting of vermillion red, black and cream, demand attention and visitors see it first in that display space and pause in front of it almost immediately. It was a major part of the Exhibition of Durden's work at the Keswick Museum and Art Gallery in 1958 and one of the paintings recorded in Mr Tom Wilson's minute of June 19th, 1958 as presented to the Museum "on permanent loan". It formed a magnificent centrepiece for the November 2021 Exhibition at the same venue, drawing similar attention and acclaim.

In the painting Betty is wearing a knee length dress in a cream material which is decorated with prominent frills across the skirt. The cream colour has a pinkish hue. She is seated on an impressive white bearskin rug reading a book or pamphlet. He legs are tucked underneath her to the left hand side, thus displaying stylish pink satin heeled shoes. Her weight is supported by her right elbow resting on the head of the bear. Much of the impact comes from the accompanying props; a red draped throw at her side on which rests a black hat with a gold tassel and a dark backdrop of a decorated curtain, which occupies nearly two thirds of the painting. The effect is theatrical on many levels. The distinctive fabric has a prominent abstract motif of red flowers, creating a semicircular pattern, possibly on two separate curtains that are drawn together to complete an oval

The Bridesmaid
Keswick Museum and Art Gallery

shape. In true Durden fashion this pattern is further highlighted by what appears to be a slim shaft of sunlight. It creates a magnificent background for the elegant and beautiful Betty, relaxing with a book or booklet in her left hand and using her right hand to turn the pages. The reading material appears to be a prop and she is looking directly at her father. Even the polar bear looks at ease with open eyes looking away to the right. It is one of Durden's most well known paintings and still draws much interest and discussion.

I was intrigued as to why Durden had given this painting the title of *The Bridesmaid*. In time it became known simply as 'Betty', but there was no escaping the fact that originally Durden called it *The Bridesmaid*. Had Betty ever been a bridesmaid? Was there any resemblance between this painting and her appearance if she ever fulfilled this role? The outfit certainly looked suitable as a bridesmaid's dress.

Miraculously, the *Lancashire Daily Post* in the summer of 1926 came up with a clue if nor the complete answer. Betty was indeed a bridesmaid at the wedding of her cousin, Madeleine Ellis on June 2nd 1926. Madeline was *the eldest daughter of Mr J. V. Ellis of Calva House, Workington, the Manager of the United Steel Company's properties in West Cumberland and a director of the company.* She married *Mr George Augustus L. Helder, son of Mr L.T. Helder, clerk to the Whitehaven Magistrates* at St John's Church, Workington. Her bridesmaids were her sisters, Denise and Yvonne and her cousin Betty Durden. The newspaper carried the headline *PRETTY WEST CUMBERLAND WEDDING* and the reporter assiduously described many details of that significant day assessing, probably correctly, that this would turn out to be the wedding of the year.

So along with her cousins Denise and Yvonne, Betty was indeed a bridesmaid in 1926. The detailed description of the dresses given in the *Lancashire Daily Post* reflects the importance of the occasion and it is very likely these outfits would be at the cutting edge of fashion that summer. However it seems unlikely that the description of the dress worn as a bridesmaid accurately matched the dress in the painting but perhaps the cream and champagne colours of the fabrics bear some resemblance to each other.

Betty was 18 when she was bridesmaid at that fashionable June wedding in Cumberland. She fulfilled that role again 4 years later in 1930 at the wedding of Denise when her cousin married Harry Grice. Janet was able to forward me a photograph of that wedding and it's interesting to see Betty in a different light. The photograph shows the bride and groom and 4 bridesmaids. Presumably one is the Matron of Honour, Mrs Madeleine Helder and one of the others is Yvonne, Denise's other sister. Betty features on the far right of the picture and looks poised and elegant. They all carry lateral sheaves of flowers showing what look like long stemmed blooms possibly of lupins or delphiniums and wear matching gowns and small brimmed hats. These hats are all worn at a 45 degree angle giving the ladies rather a jolly but sophisticated look on what was obviously a happy occasion. The bride carries a cascading bouquet of white flowers which appear to be roses. The photograph is in black and white, so it's difficult to ascertain the colour of the dresses, but they are in a light shade so could possibly be white or cream or a very pale pastel shade. They are full length with short or inset sleeves and a triple ruche detail from mid calf to the hem. The picture is completed by the best man and two children. The little flower girl, also in a full length dress, carries a small posy and the rather less enthusiastic looking page boy is in the customary long fashionable trousers.

So did Durden take Betty's role at his niece Madeleine's wedding as any sort of inspiration for his spectacular iconic painting. Denise's wedding took place after the completion of the painting so any connection would have to with Madeleine's ceremony. Her wedding was in 1926 and the painting was completed in 1927 so maybe the champagne and cream colours of the fabric formed some sort of inspiration for the Bridesmaid painting.

It's all an interesting and probably imaginative conjecture, but as long as that title, given by Durden himself, remains in place the conundrum remains open to discussion. Whatever the unknown context *The Bridesmaid* remains a fascinating painting.

12: Fame

By the mid 1920's, Durden was painting extensively and successfully. He now had the facilities and space he needed in the environment he valued from both an artistic and commercial point of view. Millbeck Place gave the family a permanent home in Cumberland and Durden was able to develop an outside barn/coach house into a useful studio. Here he was surrounded by his beloved Lake District and the house and studio nestled in the tranquility and quiet routine of the peaceful village and farming community. The splendour of the western fells was on his doorstep. He sold the iconic *Summer in Cumberland* painting to Manchester Art Gallery in 1926 and was elected to the Royal Institute of Oil Painters that same year. He was awarded the prestigious Sliver Medal from the Societie des Artistes Francais in Paris in 1927.

At some point possibly in the 1930's, Durden rented a property in Ladbroke Square, London. The downstairs became a living area and a studio and the second floor a useful flat. This flat was let to a Kathleen Iris Meredeith and whilst living there she met Joe, the adventurous and talented son of the Durden family. The couple married in 1938.

A delightful and informative black and white photograph shows Durden at his easel painting in Ladbroke Square. With the inevitable pipe clamped between his teeth, he is a picture of concentration as he paints a full length portrait of Betty. She is standing on the balcony shown through the open French

Lady with a Fan

windows and the light falls across her long dress and fashionable wide brimmed hat. The easel is at an angle to the camera so the resulting portrait isn't revealed. Ruby, also with her back to the camera, relaxes in a chair at the side of the window with her feet up on a low stool and appears to be concentrating on some sewing or embroidery. In the 27th May, 1931, issue of the 'Queen' magazine the critic comments on Royal Academy pictures exhibited at Burlington House. One of the ones he most liked was *A Balcony In Kensington* by Mr James Durden.

Between 1923 and the early 1930's Durden was also showing paintings at the Royal Academy, the Royal Institute of Oil Painters, The Lakes Artists Society at Tullie House in Carlisle, Manchester Art Gallery and other Art Galleries. Many of these paintings were singled out for critical acclaim particularly by the Northern newspapers. The Yorkshire Post, The Birmingham Post, The Manchester Guardian, The Liverpool Post and Mercury and the Northern Echo all comment, mostly favourably on Durden's work. They are joined by national titles: the Times, the Daily Telegraph, the Observer, the Morning Post, The Spectator and specialist Art magazines such as the Connoisseur and The Outlook. The Archive gave me access to all these cuttings because a firm called Durrants was commissioned to collect ephemeral references to Durden paintings and reviews. There is no indication of the instigator here but I'm guessing it was his agent Enid Balchin or maybe Ruby. There are 34 cuttings from brief references to more detailed descriptions. So the Yorkshire Post on the 23rd May1925, looking at an Exhibition of Northern Artists observes : *Mr James Durden's Black and Gold is a portrait amid decorative accessories, the gold background in Chinese style being effectively treated.*

The Birmingham Post on the 30th April 1927 identifies the Durden entry to the Royal Academy and this one is a familiar

110

painting: *Mr James Durden's 'Betty', a large and lively canvas in which the painter has tackled all sorts of technical problems with cheerful courage and has come through a severe test of his capacities with flying colours. His picture is undeniably a piece of frank and uncompromising realism, but it is conspicuously well done.*

The East Cumberland News reviews the Lakes Artists Society Exhibition at Tullie House in Carlisle on the 6th December,1924. The anonymous reviewer confines his remarks to 'Lakes scenes by Lakes Artists': *Mr James Durden contributes both oils and watercolours. His Cumberland Mountains (no 83) representing Bassenthwaite Lake and hills, has charming pearly greys in the distance, which is thrown back by the strength in the trees in the nearest part. His oils are much bolder in treatment and his 113 gives us the impression of sunshine and shadow, such as we associate with a west wind in the Lakes.*

Unfortunately the paintings are only identified by number and not by recognisable title.

It's difficult not to sidetrack whilst studying these flimsy and original press cuttings to pick out the references to Durden. On their own they provide a remarkable contemporary history of Art in the 1920s and would be a fascinating source of material for any art historian. Durden was exhibiting works next to those of other notable artists such as W.G.Collingwood and Walter Sickert. In the cutting from the Daily Telegraph on the 15th June 1926, R. R. Tatlock reviews the exhibits in the Royal Academy: *Mr Walter R Sickert's oddly entitled 'Death and the Maiden' is neither one of his best nor one of his most characteristic pictures, and it is atrociously hung besides works with which it has nothing whatever in common. The amazing beauty and reticence of its colour and the sensitiveness and refinement of its form is utterly blasted in that environment. The truth is that it is not the sort of picture for a Royal Academy Exhibition, but having accepted it,*

111

the hanging committee ought to have done it better justice.

Durden gets a brief commendation in this article for his painting of the Artist's Family. However it is worth noting that he had paintings accepted in the prestigious Royal Academy Exhibitions nearly every year between 1923 and 1930, but was never awarded an R.A.

It's also interesting to see that Durden's old friend is also exhibiting at this time. Walter Webster is singled out for commendation by the Art critic of the Birmingham Post reviewing the exhibition of the Royal Institute of Oil Painters in October 1927. He comments: *Of much importance also, are Mr W.E. Webster's dainty and brilliantly accomplished figure picture, 'Rose leaves when the rose is dead'.*

Even L.S Lowry makes an appearance. In the Manchester Guardian of April (the year was missing) the headline reads: *An Export of Art* and the extract says: *The success of Manchester paintings in submission to the Royal Academy has been noted lately, from day to day in the 'Court and Personal' column of the paper. A further list may now be given of Painters whose works are being hung in the Paris Salon, which opens on Sunday. Mr L.S. Lowry has had two oil paintings accepted, one of a football match, the other of a street scene composed about a baker's van. One wonders what Paris will make of Mr Lowry.*

Durden also has two oil paintings accepted, but they are not identified.

Summer in Cumberland also made an Academy appearance, before it was sold to Manchester Art Gallery. In a lengthy report (unidentified, undated newspaper), Frank Rutter walks round Gallery 5 and sees the painting. He comments: *the painting shows a gracious interior with a wide expanse of landscape seen through a window, has much charm in its delicate sunny colour and general arrangement.*

In 1933, when Betty married Leon, it was thought that Cape

Town would provide a good opportunity for Durden's paintings to reach a wider audience and the family took with them enough pictures to mount an Exhibition. This Exhibition opened in December 1933 at Ashbeys's Galleries on Church Street, Cape Town. It was reviewed by Art critic Melvin Simmers for the Cape Times on December 8th under the headline
MR JAMES DURDEN'S EXHIBITION PICTURES WITH LITERARY FLAVOUR REALISM AND SLICK TECHNIQUE

> **An English Painter at Ashbey's**
>
> *James Durden's Exhibition Next Month*
>
> Mr. James Durden, R.O.I., a notable English painter whose work is well known at the Academy and at the Paris Salon, is now in Cape Town, and will hold an exhibition of his work at Ashbey's Galleries from December 7. The exhibition will remain open for about three weeks.
> Mr. Durden is particularly noted as a painter of portraits and of interiors, and he has some very beautiful examples of both these types of work to show next month. He has the silver medal for portrait group gained at the Paris Salon.
> His landscape work is also of fine quality. He spends much of his time

Frustratingly there is no indication of which pictures Mr Simmers is actually viewing and it sounds as if he is equally irritated by the fact that he had no catalogue. Consequently the paintings are referred to by numbers. Whilst acknowledging the slick technique used in the paintings Mr Simmons is rather dismissive of what he refers to as Durden's literary approach: *The artist has a decided literary outlook and serves up in an attractive manner little bits and pieces of sentimental pseudo-romanticism. They are primarily illustrations of some trifles of life in fancy dress. . . .* Ouch!

However he tempers this criticism with a suggestion that: *Mr Durden's technical grasp is worth more serious depth of subject*' and acknowledges that the artist has sensitive perceptions of tonal values.

The landscapes are received with more approval: *The chief joys of the whole show are the landscapes, which are at variance with the impression that the artist has reached the zenith of his own particular form of expression. They are entirely delightful and devoid of the vulgarity which pervades all the figure pieces.*

113

They have simplicity and bear evidence of aesthetic vision which I had thought somewhat absent from the larger compositions.

This seems a little harsh and the use of the word 'vulgarity' soon caused an interesting furore.

He commends the colour used in the smaller exhibits as: *more beautifully restrained and moving than the obvious contrasts of magenta, viridian and yellow used in the figure compositions.*

His final comments rather question Durden's taste: *It is extraordinary to me that one who has moments of through-seeing into the beautiful such as in the paintings of these landscapes and in that of the figure and drapery in No.19 can be overruled so often by questionable taste.*

However he concludes the pictures are astonishingly well carried out, the surface quality being consistent throughout, and the exhibitionis interesting in that it shows what can be done in the way of realism by a successful painter.

The same Exhibition was either remounted, repeated or still in situ on February 5th to the 10th of the following year. This time a catalogue has been preserved and 31 paintings are numbered and listed. Some are easily identifiable. No 2 is *The Artist's Family* and it looks as if Mr Simmons' criticism may refer to that painting: *The tones in number 2 are very closely observed especially in the lower portions of the picture, though I cannot understand why the artist made such a bad slip as in the strident blue of the flowers and in the rather unsure figure of the girl, leaning on the table.*

He is obviously not aware of Durden's predilection to his favourite cobalt blue!

Fantasy is there, as is *Morning* and *Betty and Chu*. It would appear that Durden must have painted some more landscapes whilst in South Africa. Two refer to Table Mountain and three to Welgelegen. This latter refers to a pleasant area of Cape Town,

Jeunesse et Soleil

boasting parks, guest houses and hotels some with views of Table Mountain. In fact two of these paintigs are interiors with one called *The Dining Room*. Another one is entitled *The Honeysuckle Hedge*, so plainly Durden had enough materials with him to commit to an extended stay with some idea of a Cape Town Exhibition. 29 of the works are listed as oil paintings and two *The Blue Ocean* and *Camps Bay* as watercolours.

The next newspaper review appeared a week later in The Cape on December 15th. This time the headline was
TWO PICTURES EXHIBITIONS
and Mr Bernard Lewis described the works of an Edward Roworth and James Durden.

His opening paragraph immediately ackowledges Durden's skill and versatility: *I think there has never been in Capetown a one-man show of such decorative portraits as Mr J.Durden is now exhibiting at Ashbey's Galleries. He come to us with a big reputation. I have seen reproductions in colour of his portraits and interiors in many overseas art magazines and illustrated papers, and now two dozen of his beautiful oil paintings tell me that he is indeed a sensitive artist with an astonishing facile brush.*

It looked as if this review was getting off to a celebratory start but it goes on to be somewhat less than enthusiastic and comments that: *Durden's sense of decoration was not instinctive, was perhaps a little mannered; that his predilection for flat, clear spaces of a more or less unbroken tone was in danger of becoming an affection* [sic].

He develops this observation: *there is a certain seductive languor in Mr Durden's portraits which may easily descend to listlessness and laxity . . . The velvet glove is there, but not the iron hand.*

The following paragraph identifies some specifc pictures in the Exhibition and the portraits receive somewhat better treatment. He also comments on 4 interiors which are arrestingly beautiful. *Morning*, which is undoubtedly the *June Morning* owned by Keswick Museum, is applauded for the use of light and tone: *Misty sunshine floods the room, enfolding the blonde hair of the girl, the white and green caps* (misprint here ... does he mean cups?) *filling all the room with a soft, and tender light.*

The article doesn't end well as he concludes with the comment: *but it really is impossible to describe a picture one admires; it is far easier to pick to pieces a picture one dislikes.*

So taken as a whole these are not particularly good reviews. However, interestingly enough other Art critics came to Durden's defence. In an undated cutting a critic identified only as 'F.W.G'. commented: *To an artist whose pictures have been on several occasions accepted by and prominently hung at the Royal Academy and have won medals at the Paris Salon, I don't suppose it matters very much what Mr Melvin Simmers says or thinks about them, but when a journal of the standing of the Cape Times permits its critics to accuse Mr Durden of 'vulgarity in all the figure pieces' I do think it is going a good way beyond the realms of fair criticism.*

He concludes his article: *I consider that the Cape Town public have been given the opportunity of viewing perhaps the best individual collection which has ever been displayed in this city and I do hope they will not be put off by the faint praise of Mr Simmers and will avail themselves to the fullest extent do the opportunity of seeing some really first class pictures by an artist who ranks high abroad.*

It almost looks as if a full scale row erupts now as a Mr Herbert Penny joins in. He admits he didn't see the Simmers report, but has read the F.W.G. article. He is outraged at the use of such terms as 'vulgarity'. He goes further *In fact I consider such an accusation so cruel and unjust that it could well have been deliberately calculated to influence art lovers to remain* away from Mr Durden's exhibition. He further adds that I envy Mr Simmers his facile flow of artistic terms, but am thankful that my idea of what is vulgar is entirely opposed to that of Mr Simmers.

Such a spirited artistic debate can only have enhanced the interest in the Durden Exhibition. To quote the old journalistic maxim about no such thing as bad publicity.

The final accolade comes from Mr Penny: *In conclusion, I should be glad if one or more of Mr Durden's works could find a permanent home in Cape Town's Art Gallery in place of some which in my humble opinion are truly vulgar, course specimens of so-called Art.*

In the Garden

So it would appear that Durden emerged from the Cape Town experience with his reputation intact and indeed rather enhanced. His name was now certainly well known in artistic circles and the critical debate in the media brought his work to the attention of the general public.

As we know Durden was a rather retiring and self-effacing man and he never actively sought any fame or public acclaim. One of his friends commented that the idea humorously expressed by Lord Beaverbrook was applicable to Durden

> *He who whispers down a well,*
> *About the things he has to sell ;*
> *Will never make as many dollars*
> *As he who climbs a hill and hollers.*

However it seems Durden was prepared to exhibit his work on home territory and here he fared somewhat better than he had in South Africa. In February 1951, 27 of his paintings were exhibited in Whitehaven Public Library. The subjects covered a range of material featuring local landscapes from the Solway, Howgate, the Derwent Valley, Moresby, St Bees and Whithaven. Further locations included Richmond Park, Windsor, Cornwall, Pas de Calais and CapeTown. In the title for this exhibition these are all described as from the private collection of James Durden R.O.I.

Durden was of course well known in Whitehaven because of his design of the War Memorial and the bronze and enamel War Memorial plaque in Moresby Church. The Exhibition was reviewed by an anymous journalist in the Whitehaven News on February 15th. Here Durden is described as *a distinguished landscape painter, poster designer and book illustrator.*

The review starts well: *The atmosphere of the present exhibition is that of quiet dignity and grace. The artist's style reveals a very soft and gentle blending of colours and and a diligent attention to detail, light and shade.*

However *this charm and technical skill* is criticised for *the absence of vitality and conviction. The pictures are, as it were, almost too beautiful.* The landscapes selected for special mention are *Sheep Shearing* but this is described as: *a rustic scene posterlike in its barrennes*s, and the lovely water colour of *Barngill Beck* and the fragrant beauty of *Anstey's Cove.*

The Exhibition was opened by a Mr Ormrod who welcomed his old friend whom he described as almost a West Cumbrian.

Durden was President of the Keswick Society of Art and this exhibition showcased the talents of several well known local artists. There was an impressive range of watercolours with an understandable local appeal. The Braithwaite farmer Mr Martin Henderson shows a distinctive style in the use of colourful and striking light effects and Dick Fisher, the Keswick climber also exhibits work in water colours and a notable piece of sculpture in wood *Prayer.*. Mr E.G.Sarsfield-Hall submitted a number of paintings of foreign scenes. This is the brother of Carol Sarsfield-Hall whose family purchased Skiddaw Lodge after the Ellis family left. They remained friends with Ruby and it seems likely that Carol was responsible for the erection of the headstone for Leonard and Betty Green in Crosthwaite churchyard. Edward Sarsfield-Hall had a distinguished military career before he was killed in action in Crete on the 29th May,1941. Miss Anderson of Common Hill has two beautiful old style watercolours of The Tower Crosthwaite Church, and Fellside Cottage. Three of Durden's paintings are also mentioned. *Inspiration*, *Fireworks in Keswick* and *Spring Flowers*, which is almost three dimensional in the way the flowers seem to stand out of the picture as though they were real.

The next Exhibition of a Durden collection that I have selected to highlight took place in Septmber of 1952 at the Fitz Park Museum and Art Gallery. This was an interesting event as several people involved in its presentation appear to have separate agendas.

Firstly it looks as if the Fitz Park Trust were instrumental in instigating this Exhibition. Mr Tom Wilson, a fascinating character with an impressive record of care and concern for the town, was a member of the Trust and was on the Board of the Keswick Museum and Art Gallery. At some point he appeared to almost fall out with the Trust because as he pointed out in the Herald on September 13th 1952 ... The Art Gallery was built to foster art in Keswick and district, but unfortunately the scenes laid before the Trustees for a permanent art gallery had not been carried out because of the ever increasing demands for recreational facilities in the park. The idea of setting aside money to acquire pictures was now impossible because their funds were exhausted, so they would have to depend on gifts and legacies.

The indefatigable Tom Wilson took himself up to Millbeck to talk to Mr Durden and see the contents of the studio. From there he suggested that the people of Keswick ought to have an opportunity of seeing them. Mr Durden thought that Keswick people would not be interested but he (Mr Wilson) persuaded him that they would be …..

The 1952 Exhibition was the result. At the opening Mr Wilson explained all this context and further commented that seeing these things of beauty would benefit children, local students and ordinary people. Obviously not one to miss an opportunity he went on to say that he hoped the trustees would make an effort get something from that collection not only as a notable addition to the Art Gallery, but also in memory of a great artist who lived among them.

The Catalogue of that 1952 Exhibition lists 61 paintings that came from Millbeck Place to the Gallery that early September. It was described as part of the collection in the Studio which must have been packed to the rafters with paintings and I would have loved to have seen Tom Wilson's face as he entered the barn!

It would appear that the other person with a hidden agenda may have been Durden himself. According to two of the reviews, the paintings were to be dispersed after the Exhibition as the artist was going to live with his son in America. Obviously Durden didn't go to America as planned and Ruby's death in 1958 became the catalyst for the acquisition of the Durden legacy. Durden was very clear that this permanent loan was made as a memorial to Ruby. The arrangement was that the paintings could never be sold by the Museum. However, after her fathers's death Betty laid claim to and removed Grasmere and Sheep Shearing.

The West Cumberland Times for Saturday, September 13th headlined the Exhibition with LAST LOOK AT LAKE ARTIST'S PAINTINGS and PROVOST OF ETON OPENS KESWICK EXHIBITION. The provost of Eton was Mr Claude Elliott OBE, MA and the exhibition opened with some considerable ceremony and several speeches. Mr Elliott described it as *a collection rarely seen outside one of the large cities.*

The landscapes received particular praise and I loved the rather naive but great comment about the paintings and the spectators. They were happy pictures and they were very happy to have a chance of seeing them. A further comment I couldn't resist quoting: *Mr Durden was not one of those artists who puzzled the viewer as to what his pictures actually represented, or made one wonder if they were hung the right way up, and unlike some modern paintings they did not give rise to any dark suspicion of leg-pulling on the part of the artist.*

    This local Exhibition was very well received in the town and the county. The 61 paintings covered Durden's range and considerable versatility and portraits, landscapes at home and abroad, buildings from farms and cottages to grand Venetian towers, gardens, streams and becks, coasts and seascapes, mountains, lakes, flowers, trees, fantasy and family all earn accolades and compliments. It is interesting to see that some of the paintings featured in other exhibitions. The Welgelegan pictures are there and the Paris silver medal family painting and several of Betty including Betty and Chu. Fantasy and Dresden China, also known as The Flower Group or A Mixed Bunch made the sea journey out to South Africa and back again. These are large paintings and transport logistics must have been interesting. It also bears out the theory that Ruby was reluctant to part with her husband's paintings. Several Italian pictures are exhibited featuring Capri, Venice, Ischia, and Naples and some Cornish landscapes. Predictably the local landscapes were particularly appreciated by both the public and the press.

    There was another smaller exhibition in Keswick in July and August 1987, but this was a posthumous presentation with only 6 of the 1952 pictures on display. The rest of the paintings came from private collections. Durden also exhibited in Australia, Vienna, Canada and New Zealand. I have chosen to feature the Cape Town and Keswick exhibitions, not only because of the critical analysis, but because of the interesting subtexts and opinions involved from other parties.

Lady in a Purple Dress

13: Portraits and People

Commissions for portraits developed s Durden's reputation grew. These portraits were usually pictures of ladies and it seems likely that a gentleman would commission Durden to paint a (possibly flattering) picture of his wife, daughter or family. This was a successful way of them showing off their wealth and prosperity. Durden was able to provide the props and theatrical settings to complement the subject and the work was completed in his studio. In time they became treasured as family heirlooms. Some were exhibited before being delivered and some eventually found their way into Art Galleries and Auction Houses, but generally they disappeared into private homes.

Frustratingly names often disappeared, so a title like *The Green Sunblind* is not very informative. It was shown at the Royal Academy in 1921 and was reproduced in the *Studio Magazine* on November 14th, 1928. It's a delightful full length portrait of a young lady posed predictably in front of a green sunblind. She is wearing a straw sun hat and a dark blue long sleeved summer dress. An open book sits on the sofa next to her, but plainly her most recent activity has been the picking of a colourful selection of garden flowers now in the basket in her hand. It's a delightful painting, but the subject does not appear to be Betty or Ruby and there is no indication of her identity.

Of course some of these portraits were not commissions, but simply created by Durden using known or unknown models. However, Durden primarily used his daughter and sometimes his wife as his models and Betty was painted many times.

Access to these portraits is understandably limited, but there is no doubt that Durden was a prolific figure painter, often giving

The Green Sunblind shown at Royal Academy in 1921

The Mountaineer: The Artist's Son

his subjects a flamboyant and theatrical background. Some of these portraits reflected an affluent society showing light filled elegant interiors. Portraits featuring Betty and Ruby are recognisable. Some were kept by the family or subsequently sold. In some cases portraits were bequeathed to art galleries as in the case of Keswick with the Brown family portrait going to Manchester Art Gallery. Possibly the first portrait to appear in the public arena was the one of the 7 year old Betty which was exhibited in the Royal Academy in 1915 and reviewed favourably by the *Newcastle Journal* on the 5th May.

Durden also painted a striking portrait of his son Joseph. Joseph Valentine Ellis was born in 1910 and died in 1998. Joe spent some time in Switzerland at the Alpine School there and Betty joined him in 1928 where she discovered and developed her interest and skill in skiing.

Joe was an enthusiastic mountaineer and the portrait highlights this aspect of his activities. It's called *The Artist's Son* or sometimes *The Mountaineer*. It appeared in the Phillips auction in 1998 and is now in private hands, so my only view of this painting is a black and white photograph. It shows Joe as a young man seated on a mountain ledge with an impressive arête in mid distance behind him. This leads to a steep and precipitous twin summit partly obscured by wisps of cloud particularly characteristic of high mountain regions. Joe is shown wearing a heavy jacket and equipped with a haversack on his back and a climbing rope hanging from his waist. A slight turn of the body means that his head and shoulders are at an angle from the painter and consequently his face is in profile. It's a strong face with a slightly aquiline nose and an assertive chin. He appears to be totally absorbed in the area around him and the expression on his face indicates complete concentration and determination. Here is a young and fit climber with an impressive set of skills, completely at ease and confident in this dangerous environment.

This 'dangerous environment' may have been in Switzerland, but could also have been in the Drakensberg Mountains in South Africa. Joe was a pioneer and explorer with a keen interest in botany. He inherited his father's creative talent and became a gifted cine-biologist. He was a respected and acknowledged expert in the highly specialised work of microbiology, making a number of films for Gaumont British called *Secrets of Nature*. He was a member of the 1935 expedition to Basutoland (present-day Lesotho) hunting for rare plants. This was led by Helen Milford, a respected horticulturalist of the period. Helen Milford was convinced many new and undiscovered alpine plants were growing in the higher regions of South Africa. She was accompanied by only two other experts, Barbara Hussey and Joseph Durden. During that time Joe photographed over 800 rare specimens in situ on what was a challenging and exciting expedition.

The details were documented by Joe and his written record also contained photographs and maps. The intention was to produce a book as well as a series of lectures all of which would bring in retrospective funding for the expedition. However, the project was overtaken by the war and the manuscript diary lay unused and unpublished. Some time later Joe started to write his version of the expedition, but sadly it was never finished and it fell to his daughter and granddaughter to pick up this story.

So thanks to the next generations, the contents of Joe's little red book appeared in a rather different format years later. His granddaughter Catherine Jennifer Hey, (Jenny) and Janet flew to South Africa in 2001 to retrace much of Joe's 1935 expedition. With all Joe's previous material on hand, they reconstructed the context, matching his photographs with the scenery, consulting his descriptions and following much of his journey in somewhat less hazardous circumstances. Joe's enthusiastic record of the expedition, recorded its successes and failures, and in his case, some rather hair raising adventures. On January 29th 1935, he climbed Cathkin Peak in the Drakensbergs, and was benighted on the way down. He spent the night on an 18 inch ledge in total darkness, rain, mist, bitterly cold wind and thunderstorms without support or pony transport.

On Jenny's return, she produced a fascinating book called *High Garden*, interspersing Joe's original text with her own parallel experiences of the trip. Using her own diaries she created a series of fictitious letters home to her (now deceased) grandfather. This cleverly structured device succeeded in bringing to life the account that was meant to be written, so many years previously. The illustrations created from Joe's negatives and her own brilliant specimen colour photographs make this a captivating book. I really enjoyed the adventure story and the suspense created by the intrepid Joe and his exciting escapades.

Jenny's grandfather would have been very proud of his granddaughter and this excellent tribute to his expedition.

Within months of his return from the Milford expedition Joe became editor, director and scriptwriter of biological educational films for Gaumont British Instructional Film Ltd and made over 50 films, becoming an expert in time-lapse photography. It was a highly successful career but his love of plants and mountains remained with him all his life and his portrait painted by his father captures the essence of Joe Durden .

There is also a painting of Joe's wife, but again this is in private hands and I only have access to another black and white photographs, Kathleen Iris Meredith was born in 1908 and died in 1985. The couple met when Kathleen was renting the flat above the Studio in Ladbroke Square. The portrait is presented in a similar format to the Mountaineer picture. Kathleen is seated on the arm of a chair or settee with the half turn at the waist again producing a strong profile. The short curly hair and half smile give the impression of a pleasant and attractive young lady, again very much at ease with herself and her surroundings. No flowing gowns or theatrical backgrounds in this painting. It looks as if Kathleen is wearing slacks, but they could actually be jodhpurs and certainly this young lady's dress suggests riding and outdoor activity. The outfit is completed by a long sleeved shirt and tie. The left hand rests on the back of the seat and the right hand, draped casually across her lap, holds a riding crop. She is accompanied by a hound of some variety, who sits fully alert behind her left knee. Again he is in profile and the black and white markings emphasise the concent-ration shown by this hun-

Fantasy
Keswick Museum and Art Gallery

ting dog. His mouth is partially open with an impression of slight panting and recent activity. He is obviously well trained and totally under control, but he is almost quivering with excitement. There are not many animals in Durden paintings, but his practice exercises at Art College indicate his skill in this area. The inclusion of Chu in the important Betty painting is an accurate and expert presentation of his own dog. As with the mountains in Joe's picture, the hunting dog in Kathleen's portrait is an appropriate accessory. We understand the significance of these backgrounds and the accurate impression they create of Durden's son and daughter in law.

As well as his commissions, Durden also used models, particularly where he was producing pictures of subjects like his flamenco dancers or simply wanted a female figure to feature in a painting. The identity of these ladies is largely unknown apart from one who featured in the November 1928 edition of *The Studio* magazine. Alongside the article by Jessica Walker

131

Stephens and a reproduction of *The Green Sunblind* there is a full page copy of a portrait called *Irene*. This very distinctive painting shows a young lady seated at a round table and posed next to an Art Deco miniature of a statue holding a bowl of fruit aloft. The dark sleeveless dress is simple and this simplicity is emphasised by the hair style. The hair is centrally parted and drawn back from the face in a severe bun or chignon. Irene rests her face against the arm of the statuette and looks away from the artist. Her expression is unsmiling, but serene and this time the background is plain with just a suggestion of a fabric drape along one edge of the picture.

The young lady in question was Irene Dineley and she was a striking and much sought out model of the time. An article in the *World's Pictorial News* of February 26th 1928 features her story. The lavish and full page spread features Miss Dineley in various poses in full length gowns or in simple profile presentations. The headlines splash with *HOW I BECAME "THE MOST PAINTED GIRL* followed by strap lines of *TOLD THAT SHE HAD PERFECT HEAD / Disheartened - Then Took Chance as Mannequin / Model Who Has Sat for Our Leading Artists / FANCY FOR STAGE'*

Once hooked into the article, the introduction goes into a brief explanation, just in case the reader was in any doubt about the identity and talents of this beautiful young lady: *A beautiful girl of Manchester, who left home to try to make her name upon the stage, Miss Irene Dineley has become famous throughout the world of art as 'the most painted girl in the country'. As she has sat for nearly a score of our most famous artists and as pictures of her have appeared three times in the Royal Academy, in the Paris Salon and in the Royal Portrait Society's shows, it may be concluded that the description does not exaggerate the facts.*

This is followed by four columns of small newsprint where Miss Dineley adopts a true story style and proceeds to entertain her readers with all the details of her humble beginnings and successful and illustrious career. She describes her 'uneventful life' to the age of 15: *I went to school, learned a lot of useless things in addition to a lot that were useful, and prepared myself*

Irene

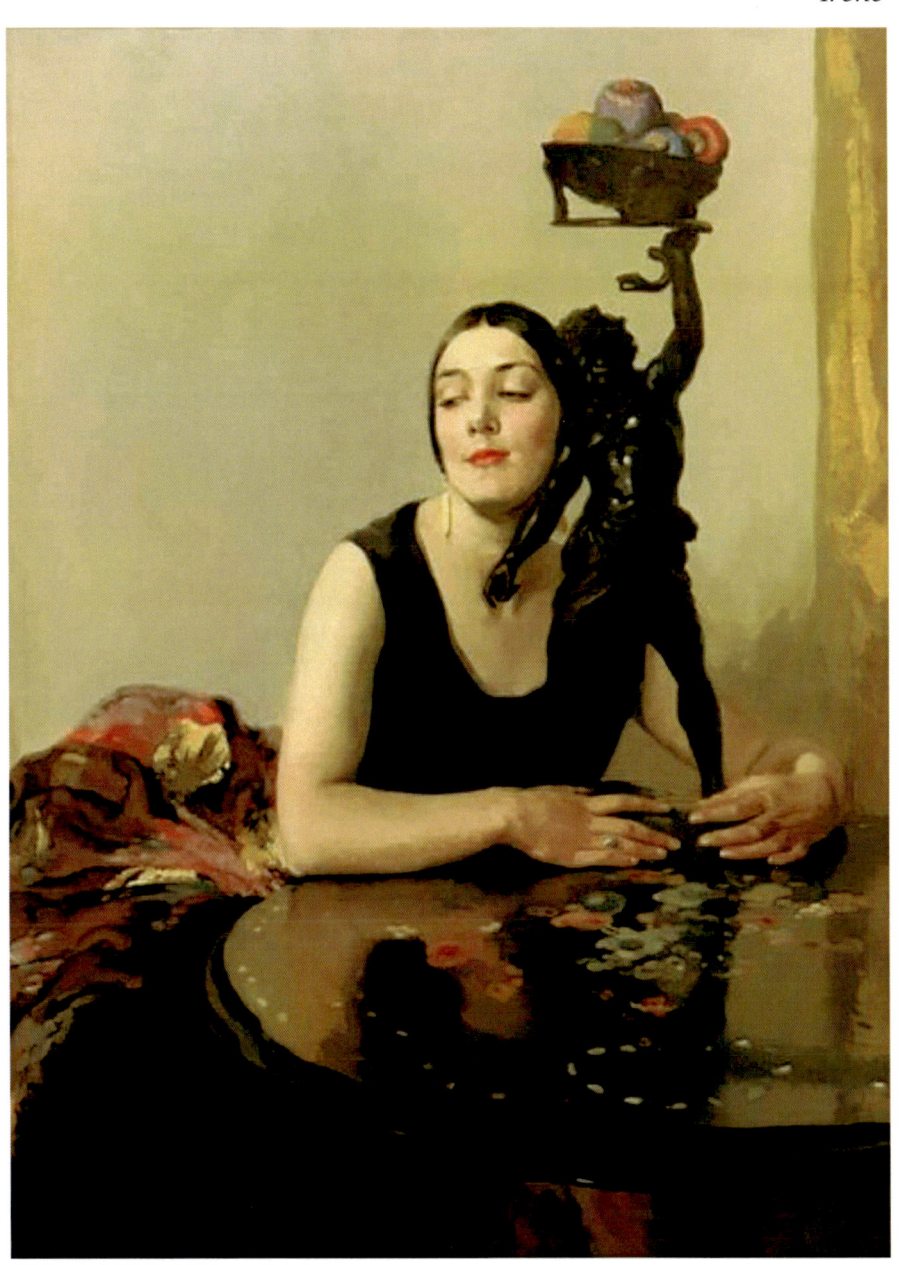

to become what the average girl eventually becomes - *a wife.*

Plainly this was not enough for the beauteous Irene. She yearned to become an actress *not so much a popular actress as a really great actress.*

She goes on to describe her parents' opposition and the suitors she turned down in favour of her thespian dream. Eventually she was allowed to go to London where friends found her a room in Russel Square and she took singing lessons at the Guildford School of Music. In spite of all her efforts and her determination (*mine was not the enthusiasm of illusion*) engagements were not forthcoming. She admits to becoming disheartened, but refuses to return to Manchester as a failure where friends might say 'I told you so'.

Fortunately rescue was on hand in the form of Lady Duff-Gordon, the famous society fashion designer, who was looking for six girls to be trained as mannequins for her forthcoming fashion parade at Murray's Club. She decreed *they must be beautiful. They must be tall and slender and they must be intelligent girls who know how to wear clothes as they should be worn . . . They must be 6 different types and I shall insist that they be girls who ha*v*e never had any previous experience of this kind.* In a "bold move" Irene called on the instigator to present herself in a self designed dress and express an interest in the scheme. There was an initial panic about her height - *You are not 5ft 9 inches* was Lady Duff-Gordon's immed-iate observation, but fortunately it was followed by *I think you will do.*

From here Irene graduated to becoming an artists' model, although she has some initial concerns: *I had always thought that people had to pay to have their pictures painted and I had never thought of them having models. Naturally I had heard of artist's models, but had always thought of them as being rather bohemian young ladies who sat in the nude and were the central figures in wild studio rags.*

However she was assured by a fellow mannequin: *"You have a wonderful head and I know a number of artists who would be glad to have you. For my head alone? I queried, and she smiled assent.*

So Irene Dineley with her perfect head continued with her career as a model and in her story she lists all the famous artists with whom she has worked. James Durden features in this list and the portrait that appeared in the Studio magazine became rather an iconic painting.

As a conclusion to the article Miss Dineley, whilst being pleased with her success, comments: *I do feel just a little proud at not having to go home without having achieved anything at all.*

However, Miss Dineley is still interested in her potential acting debut. She is proud to report that she has made a made a start understudying the leading lady in a touring production of *There's No Fool* and played one of the ladies in waiting in the film '*Madame Pompadour*' alongside the beautiful Dorothy Gish. She also played an Argentinian at the banquet given in honour of the victory over Von Spee in the film *The Battle of the Falkland Islands*. Obviously there is still all to play for and the thespian life still beckons.

Irene has a full-page tabloid spread in the *World's Pictorial News* but the bottom corner of the page is taken up by an advert (which may well prove useful to Miss Dineley in years to come !) It is an advert for a totally reliable cure for Corns. Apparently *REUDEL BATH SALTRATES* will alleviate the suffering inflicted by any sort of corns. The bath salts are dissolved in hot water and soaking your feet for 20 minutes will loosen the corns so they: *can be pulled right out, root and all, like the hull out of a strawberry. Callouses can be scraped off with the dull edge of a knife, and you will experience the joy of real foot comfort. . . . .*Ouch!

All this is endorsed by Robert Wortley, a well-known London Chiropodist who operates from 174, New Bond Street. He is happy to identify the *beneficial results* and guarantees the safety of the product.

135

The Artist's Family

Alongside commissions to paint individuals, Durden also became involved in producing family portraits. His painting of his own family won a silver medal in the Paris Salon exhibition in 1927. The central prop in this case is a long polished table situated across the middle background of the painting. The teenage Joe perches casually on one end of this table. He is wearing an open necked shirt and has one foot on the floor with the other one swinging carelessly by the table leg. In his right hand he is clutching a violin which rests across his knees with the reverse side of the instrument towards the viewer. The bow is in his other hand with the end resting across his right shoulder. The music appears to be strewn across his side of the table. His attention is taken by his mother who is seated in a chintz armchair at the other end of the table. Ruby is in fashionable dress and shoes and sports a modern bobbed hairstyle. It looks as if she has selected a drape

136

of some sort from a dark octagonal lacquer box at her feet and this decorative fabric covers her lap. Behind her is the familiar folding screen often used by Durden and beyond that a small section of the window shows part of a mature tree in full leaf. The third member of the family is posed at the same end of the table and Betty is shown in equally relaxed and casual mode. She is seated on a dining chair and rests her elbows lightly on the table, supporting her chin on her clasped hands. In front of her is a small oval decorative bowl with the familiar garden flowers and distinctive cobalt blue delphiniums. A broad brimmed sun hat is positioned next the flowers giving the impression that it had been carelessly dropped as the wearer has come in from the garden. Also on the table is a small lidded hexagonal box and closer to Ruby a small pair of scissors. It now becomes apparent that Ruby is possibly sewing or repairing the material in her hands. It's a delightful family portrait showing the members involved in the activities of a relaxing day at Millbeck Place. My thanks to Mr Peter Nelson for allowing me access to this painting .

A very similar portrait of a different family was exhibited at the Royal Academy in 1928. This was definitely a commission and it features the children of Katharine and James Brown, Nancy, Eric and Winifred. The setting looks familiar and the pIcture was indeed painted at Millbeck Place. The structure is similar to the Durden family painting with the three members of the family split with a single figure on one side of the picture and the remaining two portrayed together in an opposite position. They are closer together then the Durdens, but the approach is comparable. Fifteen year old Nancy is seated in an armchair on the left of the picture next to a small occasional table containing a flower arrangement. The flowers show the characteristic Durden favourites from the Millbeck garden with blue delphiniums, orange marigolds and white daisies. Nancy, who is wearing a fashionable knee length rather plain white dress, rests her arm lightly on the arm of the chintz chair. She appears relaxed, but does look rather posed and is not smiling. Her legs are crossed and one foot, in a dark high heeled shoe, rests on the deep red bordered carpet of the sitting room at Millbeck Place.

Winifred, Nancy and Eric, children of Mrs James Brown

Eric sits at her feet with one leg tucked under him and the other in a knee length grey sock is extended on the carpet. He looks rather a solemn little chap and was 12 years old at the time of the painting. He's wearing grey shorts and a white shirt and tie. In front of him are two playing cards and he is holding a third card in his hand. There is no indication of interest in this game and like his sister it almost looks as if he has been told not to move. These two figures occupy about half the painting and on the right hand side is 17 year old Winifred. She looks much more natural and is absorbed in reading a magazine as opposed to looking at the artist. She is depicted in profile at right angles to Durden. She too is wearing a similar white dress to her sister, but her armchair is draped rather theatrically in some flowing floral patterned material which is a typical Durden prop. Another familiar feature of a Durden portrait appears in the form of a folding screen casually placed slightly to the right behind her. The Chinese figure and landscape on this panel are predominantly a burnt orange ochre colour and pick up the shades of the carpet.

I am most grateful to Mr Alan Mathewson of Gullane for providing me with the contextual details of this painting. This delightful gentleman is Nancy's son and he was able to tell me how he and his late wife inherited the picture and later donated it to Manchester Art Gallery. Originally it had a heavy gold leaf ornamental frame, which was tending to fragment, so the family had it reframed with the existing minimalist frame.

The story of the figures in the painting is a fascinating one and Mr Mathewson was able to share details of his family history. His grandmother was Katharine (Kitty) Baines who was born in Leicester in 1879. She married James Brown in 1908 but her husband died in Bournemouth in 1920 possibly as a result of mustard gas poisoning from World War One. Tragically he never saw his children as the teenagers they are in the painting.

Mr Mathewson's mother was Nancy who was born in West Hartlepool in 1912. She married Arthur Mathewson in 1940. Arthur's father was a doctor and he lived in Keswick. Dr John Mathewson's surgery was at 37, Brundholme Terrace, only doors away from Keswick Museum and Art Gallery.

Like his grandfather James Brown, Eric too became a victim of war. Eric is shown as a 12 year old boy in the centre of the painting. He was killed at Arnhem in 1944. The older daughter Winifred, who was born in 1910, married Ralph Denby. She died at East Grinstead in Sussex in 1959 after contracting cancer.

I travelled to Manchester Art Gallery in January 2022 to see this painting and of course 'Summer in Cumberland'. This latter painting was on display but the Brown portrait was in store at the time. I am most grateful to Hannah Williamson, the Curator of Fine Art who spent time with me on that exciting January morning and took me down to the depths of the Art store to see this very impressive picture. It has been preserved in perfect condition and the colours are magnificent with the rusts and vermillion shades of the Chinese background screen and the carpet. I was also struck by the cobalt blue of the familiar delphiniums from the Millbeck Place garden. The painting is available to view on request. It's gratifying to think that this northern city which first cultivated the artistic talent of the young

Durden now has two of his most iconic paintings.

As a final representation of Durden's portraits, I'm going to feature one of my favourite paintings . It's quite a small picture owned by one of the Museum Trustees, Mr John Temple. He purchased this picture at auction and I'm grateful for his permission to use it as a reproduction in this chapter. It was presented as an unidentified lady with no date, but has the authentic Durden signature. Mr Temple has subsequently suggested that it could be described as *The Pianis*t or simply *A Lady in Blue*.

It shows a young lady seated at a polished dark wood grand piano. Her left hand rests lightly on the keyboard and she has stopped playing to turn her head to face Durden. The other arm supports this gesture with her right hand slightly gripping the edge of the piano stool. The stool is covered by a gold drape which falls into the foreground of the picture. The contrast with the familiar cobalt blue of the dress is striking. The dress is deeply cut in a v at the neck, nipped in at the slim waist and features short sleeves. The fabric of the sleeves is the same blue colour, but a different material, lighter, gauzy and transparent. highlighting the shapely arms of the pianist. Her neck and part of the shoulders are also bare giving every indication of a fashionable evening dress. The outfit is complemented by a long single string of pearls which fall in a loop to rest on her lap. This simple jewellery is further emphasised by matching earrings. The lady is undeniably a beauty. She has short curly hair which is an attractive auburn shade and held in place by a black headband. Although unsmiling the facial expression is serene and confident highlighted by a vermillion red lipstick. One could be forgiven for thinking that she plays the grand piano with consummate ease and expertise. It looks as if this evening's recital or soiree will resume very shortly.

A heavy curtain takes up all the background except one small edge. This edge shows a full length window which appears to extend behind the curtain. The small strip of sky showing through the window is the same blue of the dress and accentuates the edge of the painting. This vivid blue sky might suggests a summer evening entertainment. The lower edge shows a hint of a denser landscape, which could well be a mountain or a fell and this adds

*The Pianis*t or *A Lady in Blue*
John Temple

to the perspective. The substantial curtain has a dark background with a subdued pattern of dark red flowers and green foliage. It doesn't detract from the subject in any way and the lady is thrown into dramatic relief as her blue dress contrasts with the darker shades of the heavy curtain fabric. It's a very attractive painting.

So in conclusion to this chapter we'll leave our graceful, young lady in her elegant evening gown to her soirée where she will undoubtedly captivate her audience with her charm and impress them with her skill and savoir-faire. One wonders how many suitors will emerge from the evening?

The Bathers

14: Shipwreck

As we know Durden first presented his paintings to the Keswick Museum and Art Gallery for his 1952 Exhibition. This is recorded in the Minutes of the Fitz Park Trust held on 19th June 1952. The subsequent bequest of eight pictures on permanent loan was established in 1958 after Ruby's death.

The chairman of the Trust in 1958 was Sir Percy Mirehouse Hope (1888-1972) and Keswick owes him a great deal. He was the son of a local bank manager, trained as an architect and was a tireless worker in various projects from housing and business to service on many local planning boards and committees. He had an impressive military service career in World War One, but turned down a War Office appointment in favour of returning to Keswick. He was knighted in 1954 and gave Hope Park and Lady Hope's Garden to his much loved home town.

Following his announcement at this meeting there was discussion about the value of the paintings. The Trustees were concerned about the insurance value and felt that this must be resolved before the pictures went on display. Another member of the board, Tom Wilson, was instructed to talk to Mr Durden about this.

Tom Wilson was also a well known Keswick figure. John Tomlinson Wilson, was a fascinating character with an impressive story all of his own. Born and bred in the town he involved himself in many Keswick initiatives from Crosthwaite school, Lairthwaite Secondary Modern School, the Keswick School of Industrial Arts and Crosthwaite Church where he was a contemporary of Canon Rawnsley. He is still remembered as a founder member of P.U.P.S. (the Pushing Young People's Society) raising money for local charities and projects. Their aim

DURRANT'S PRESS CUTTINGS,
St. Andrew's House, 32 to 34 Holborn Viaduct,
and 3 St. Andrew Street, Holborn Circus, E.C.I.
Telephone: CITY 4963.

Morning Post
15 Tudor Street, E.C.4.

Cutting from issue dated...... 1...7.FEB.1930..

PAINTINGS RECOVERED FROM SEA

WELLINGTON (N.Z.), Feb. 15.
Nine more pictures have been recovered from the wreck of the steamer Manuka, which foundered in a thick fog near Dunedin last December with a cargo of pictures destined for an exhibition of modern British painting to be held in New Zealand.
The newly recovered pictures are: "Down a falling Stream," by Lamorna Birch; "Moonlight off Falmouth," by Julius Olsson; "After the Bathe," by Algernon Talmage; "Land's End," by Dame Laura Knight; "The Transient Hour," by Lucy Kemp-Welch; "Fishermen at Concarneau," by Sir Matthew Thompson; "Old Nurse," by Harold Speed; "Vista," by Davis Richter; and a picture described as "an interior with chair and table before a window," which is probably the "Interior" by James Durden.—Reuter.

The pictures on board were valued at £25,000 and had been collected by Mr. Murray Fuller. Two of the pictures were by Mr. H. H. La Thangue, R.A., who died a few days after the news of the disaster was received. It was believed that his death was hastened by depression due to the loss of the pictures.

was to provide for Keswick *those things that were not provided by anyone else*. Their legacy lives on.

Tom's service life began in August 1914, when he joined the 4th Battalion of the Border Regiment.who were sent to fight in India, replacing the regular troops who were needed to fight on the Western Front. They arrived in Rangoon early in December. One of the Officers was Lieutenant Percy Mirehouse Hope, the architect from Keswick. Percy Hope and Tom Wilson must have met in very different circumstances prior to the more relaxing surroundings of serving on the Trustees of Fitz Park in 1958.

Between the 19th June 1958 and the 18th September of that same year Tom Wilson talked to Durden and raised the concerns of the Trustees about insurance. Probably in fairly typical fashion James was uncon-cerned about such matters. He airily informed Tom that many of his pictures had *travelled abroad and he had never had them insured*.

If Tom was rather taken aback by this casual approach to such matters there is no record of it. At the next Trustees meeting, Tom reported the situation and the minute simply reads *It was therefore agreed that our present cover of insurance be sufficient.*

So we now know that Durden pictures were no strangers to travel (occasionally on the high seas) and often uninsured. There is evidence that both James and Betty transported various canvasses around with them on their travels. One reason was for Exhibition Purposes and as early as 1920 when James hadn't been back long from the war, his paintings travelled to the Paris

145

A Blue Room In Kensington
Christchurch Art Gallery

Salon for display.

One painting that travelled the world had an adventure all of its own. It's an oil on canvas, 523 x 520mm, painted in 1928 called *A Blue Room in Kensington*. James was 50 by then and had acquired a London base in the form of a residence and studio at 4 Ladbroke Square in Kensington. He divided his time between his studio at Millbeck Place and Ladbroke Square and worked and painted in both places. I wondered if this painting \was done in Ladbroke Square showing a room in that house and I spent some time comparing artefacts in the painting with details from the photograph of Durden painting Betty standing on the balcony. However, my theory was quickly destroyed when Janet informed me that the Ladbroke Square studio did not have a blue room!

However further intrigue surrounds this painting. *The Morning Post* of 17th February 1930 carried a small item headed

PAINTINGS RECOVERED FROM THE SEA

and reported an incident that had taken place near Dunedin in New Zealand the previous December. This concerned a steamer called *Manuka*, a vessel of 4534 tons carrying 300 souls, a crew of 120 and a general cargo of 1700 tons. It was sailing from Melbourne, Australia to Wellington in New Zealand by way of South Island ports. The captain Ross Clerk attempted to plot a course by the Nuggets Lighthouse, but in at 11pm in darkness, a heavy swell, and thick fog, he kept the steamer too close to the shore. One passenger stated that the lookout shouted *rocks ahead* just before the *Manuka* hit the rocky ledge at Long Point. The ship was badly damaged, but the engines kept going, holding her on the rocks and with the lights still operational, the crew was able to evacuate the passengers. Even so, by the time the passengers were collected on deck the *Manuka* had a heavy list and it was almost impossible to launch a lifeboat on the port side. However it appears everyone behaved with admirable calmness and common sense. The women and children were evacuated first and within 25 minutes all the passengers were installed in the lifeboats. The departure was necessarily hurried and the unfortunate passengers abandoned ship in only the clothes they stood up in and many of the women were in nightdresses. Their adventures continued as the life boats reached a landing area at 5am with the nearest town of Owako some two miles away through bush and sheep paddocks. The townspeople came to the rescue with various forms of guidance and transport and no souls were lost. It seems the only loss was a parrot and possibly a whippet dog, although a second one came through unscathed.

 I couldn't resist a further sidetrack into this disaster, as among the passengers were members of a 12 strong theatrical company led by Miss Leonora Hogarth and Mr Leonard Doyle. The company was due to open in Dunedin with a performance of *The Family Upstairs* that week. The principals arrived in Dunedin in a car the following afternoon living up to the theatrical tradition 'the show must go on'. There was a slight problem with the loss of props, but many of these were obtained locally and some of the necessary equipment was not shipped by the *Manuka* anyway and arrived on a later ship. The company lost personal effects and souvenirs collected during the course of their tour and Mr Doyle commented that this was his first visit to New Zealand and that his entry was dramatic if unrehearsed, and he had no wish for an encore!

The point about this story comes from the Reuter's February report in the *Morning Post* where it is stated that *Nine more paintings have been recovered from the wreck of the steamer Manuka which foundered in thick fog near Dunedin last December with a cargo of pictures destined for an exhibition of modern British painting to be held in New Zealand.*

The report goes on to list the pictures: *Down by a Falling Stream* by Lamorna Birch; *Moonlight off Falmouth* by Julius Olson; *After the Bathe* by Algernon Talmage; *Lands End* by Dame Laura Knight; *The Transient Hour* by Lucy Kemp-Welch; *Fishermen at Concarneau* by Sir Matthew Thompson; *Old Nurse* by Harold Speed; *Vista* by Davis Richter; and a picture described as *An interior with chair and table before a window*, which is probably *The Interior* by James Durden'.

The report went on to inform readers that the collection was valued at £25,000 and that it also contained pictures by H.H. la Thangue, who died a few days after news of the disaster was received. It added the observation that *it was believed that his death was hastened by depression due to the loss of the pictures.*

All these paintings were collected for a proposed exhibition by Edwin Murray Fuller and his wife Mary. Together they brought six exhibitions of contemporary British Art to New Zealand. They were key players in the artistic world of Wellington from 1920 to 1945 and were renowned Art entrepreneurs in the 1930's.They travelled to Europe, Australia and England in 1926 and 1927 for the express purpose of collecting works of Art for Exhibitions in New Zealand. These were intended as mini Royal Academy exhibitions and the Academy suggested the way as to how a viewer should look at work of art .... *so that the twin academic ideals of moral purpose or educational value and beauty should be apprehended.*

Murray Fuller's contact with the influential artists of the

time was impressive, but this isn't really the arena to explore his work. He died in 1933 aged 41, leaving an impressive reputation for his Murray Fuller exhibitions as sources from which to view and purchase prestigious works of Art. His work was continued by his wife Mary. She featured a Durden painting in her 1935 Exhibition which was reviewed in the Otago Times of April 18th 1935 ...

James Durden in his 'Salute Venice' has also given us on a small canvas a beauty of atmospheric effects that will not soon be forgotten. The perfection of the shapes in the design with their flair for architectural massiveness, the blue grey colour harmony relieved judiciously by subdued warmer notes and the shimmer of hazy sunlight on water render this picture a little masterpiece of atmospheric painting.

The article goes on to describe Cundall's *Edinburgh*, but comments that it does not possess *the genius of the Durden.*

Finally we return to the intriguing question as to whether the *Interior* rescued from the Manuka was indeed *A Blue Room in Kensington*. Was the word interior just a title bestowed on it by the reporter who didn't bother to locate its correct title? I am unable to find a Durden painting with this title anywhere. What is significant is that a painting called *A Blue Room in Kensington* now hangs in Christchurch Art Gallery Te Puna O Waiwhetu in New Zealand. Investigation into its provenance reveals that it was purchased by a group of Christ Church citizens in 1932 and presented to the Art Gallery. Although always wary of jumping to conclusions, one is tempted to suggest that Edwin Murray Fuller saw the painting in England in 1928, transported it to New Zealand where it was nearly lost at sea. It then moved from Wellington to the Murray Fuller exhibition in Christchurch. Here it attracted the attention of the Christchurch public. Their judgement and generosity facilitated its permanent home in this beautiful and spectacular gallery, where it now remains, a long way from Kensington.

(Janet Durden-Hey signed a copyright agreement with the Gallery on the 3rd of March, 2012 and the Gallery signed it on the 15th March 2012).

15: The Webster Portrait Mystery

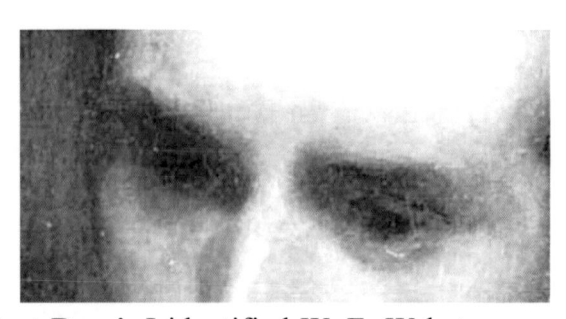

In Chapter 2 'Student Days', I identified W. E. Webster as a contemporary and lifelong friend of Durden. They were students together when James lived with the Webster family in Chelverton Road, Putney in 1901. Websster was a witness at the Durden wedding. He also attended the Royal College of Art and exhibited at the Royal Acadamy. He became a distinguished portrait panter and illustrator, painting a watercolour of the young Princess Elizabeth in 1935. In the 1911 census he was still living at home. (Interestingly, his mother Mary has the classification letter 'M' next to her name, but the enumerator has corrected himself by crossing out the 'M' and writing 'Widow above it').

Both Durden and Webster tramped Fleet Street looking for work with magazines and book publications. Both men were successful. As with Durden there is archive material of magazine covers produced by Webster with one particularly impressive one of a woman at a mirror for the magazine *Etude*. There were occasions when they were both working for the same publishers - they both had work in the *Ladies Home Journal*. They both gained a footing with book publishers as well and Webster provided some attractive illustrations for a variety of books. The *King of the Air* by Herbert Strang has four impressive colour plates executed by Webster.

Like Durden, Webster also exhibited extensively at the Royal Academy, with entries almost annually until his death in May 1959. He too was involved in The Royal Institute of Oil Painters and was awarded a Bronze medal at the Paris Salon in 1912. This was followed by Silver medals in 1913 and 1914 and a Gold medal in 1931.

Self-portrait
Walter Ernest Webster

Their paths diverged somewhat with the advent of World War One but like Durden, Webster was never in the Front Line. He didn't enlist until February 1916 and was mobilised on 6th June with a posting to the First (Reserve Garrison) Battalion of the Suffolk Regiment and later transferred to the Essex Regiment. His service records show that the Royal Engineers camouflage school tested him on the 16th September 1918 and classified him as a superior painter (as opposed to 'indifferent', 'fair' or 'skilled'). He was transferred to the Royal Engineers on the 28th September rising through the ranks from Lance Corporal in August 1916 until he became an acting Sergeant. He was never given a foreign posting and was demobilised on 18th February 1919, a fortunate survivor of the war.

Webster came home and married Susan Beatrice Pearse in the last quarter of 1919. She too was part of an artistic circle as she was a professional book illustrator. The 1919 Electoral Register records them living at Chelverton Road initially, but the following year they moved to Broome Villa at 27, Broomhouse Road near Parsons Green in London. Webster settled there for the rest of his life. He died on the 30th April,1959, the year after Ruby, so Durden lost his wife and probably his best friend in a very short space of time.

It would seem reasonable to assume that the friendship of Durden and Webster lasted until Webster's death. For most of this

A Portrait of James Durden
Walter Ernest Webster

time Durden was settled in the Lake District and Webster was in London. However, we know Durden acquired the Studio in Ladbroke Square with living accommodation, so the family spent time in London.

Both men displayed a similar artistic style. In 1920 Webster was elected a member of both the Royal Society of Painters in Water Colours and the Royal Institute of Oil Painters. He became a member of the Royal Society of Portrait Painters in 1921 and was elected Vice President of this body in 1937.

At some point he painted a portrait of James Durden. It shows James as a young man with his head turned away from the artist and looking down slightly towards the left. He is wearing a waistcoat and jacket and a thin tie. In true portrait fashion it shows his head and shoulders only. It's a sensitive portrait, portraying James with a thoughtful pensive look. Webster appears to have captured the essence of his friend and one gets the impression ithat this portrait has been painted by someone who knew his subject well. This portrait passed into the possession of Joe, James' only son, who was living in Canada and the USA.

Durden's last trip abroad was in 1963, when he and Betty went to visit Joe and family in Boston. James died in 1964 and in 1973 Joe Durden returned to England. His wife Kathleen, died in 1985 and Joe died in 1998. The Webster portrait of James Durden was left in America in 1973 with Christopher John Durden, Joe and Kathleen's son.

On February 2nd, 1975, for some reason Christopher Durden took the portrait out of the frame. Underneath the painting there was another picture. It was a head and shoulder portrait of a young lady. The neck and shoulders are bare with no jewellery. She appears to be wearing an evening dress of a light gauzy material with a puff sleeve effect and a low square neckline. The hair is swept up with a rather delicate feathering style onto the forehead. Like James, in the first portrait, she is turning slightly away from the artist and looking into the middle distance rather than down. The costume and general presentation of this figure is very typical of Webster's style. Both subjects

The Hidden Lady
Walter Ernest Webster

appear rather preoccupied with their thoughts. There is no 'smile for the camera' or direct engagement with the artist. They are both exquisite paintings done in oils on the same size canvas and give the impression of a pair. There is no date or title on either picture and so far no one has recognised the young lady.

So here is the unsolved mystery Who is the young lady hidden behind the Webster portrait of James Durden? The family have never been able to find out. This intriguing question gives rise to several theories.

Initially it was suggested by the family that the lady might be James' alter ego. Both Joe and Christopher were cross dressers and it has been considered that maybe James too, was interested in a transvestite life-style. James certainly enjoyed dressing up and enjoyed wearing extravagant costumes, but I have not been able to establish any direct evidence of serious cross dress-ing. (I'm tempted to suggest that living in a village community like ours for most of his life someone would have spotted him in the garden or on the lane if he was dressed as a lady!).

So if we look at whether the two Webster Figures show the same person it might be possible to come up with some initial tentative ideas. The poses lend themselves to a certain similarity and there is no doubt that these two figures are probably round about the same age and may have sat for Webster at roughly the same time. The faces are similar, but that may be to do with the pensive expressions which look the same. It's difficult to compare the definitive male and then female look to the portraits and gender certainly plays a function here. The features of the face are usually concerned with the depth of the forehead, the eyebrows and the eyes, the nose shape dictating the profile, the shape of the mouth and lips and the bone structure and set of the jaw forming the line of the chin. If we compare all these features one by one an opinion emerges. In the upper part of the face the forehead could be similar and the eyebrows have a slight resemblance. However the eyes are very deep set on the male and more delicately presented on the female face. The nose is much more hooked on the male and is a different shape on the female version. The lady has far more of a Cupid shape mouth, although the bottom lip does protrude in a slightly similar fashion on both faces. The line of the jaw is different.

I consulted two experts on the likelihood of this portrait showing the same person in different dress. The first, an artist and a sculptor, deliberated at length and was frustrated with only being able to see black and white photos of the portraits. He eventually concluded that the portraits show two different people. My second consultant was also an artist, but with much more knowledge about bone structure. He was definite about the structure of the jaw not being the same. He also pointed out that within the context of portrait painting it's very unlikely that a transvestite would present as the lady in the picture. She would never wear a low cut dress revealing the neck and the chest in such a way. Most transvestites wear high neck costumes often in a choker type style or with close fitting neck jewellery. He also thought that the hair was a major clue in the puzzle. If the second portrait is in fact James, then the hair must be a wig. It's unlikely that the wig would be the upswept hair style shown again revealing far more of the neck than is usual for cross dressing. Even moving the context and looking at the popular drag artists on modern media programmes, wigs normally take on long curly hair often in outrageous colours. As a final point, the delightful hair style of our mystery lady just simply doesn't look like a wig. Her beautifully dressed, slightly wavy hair is an intrinsic part of this charming portrait of an attractive figure. My second expert was in no doubt that these two paintings portray two different people. My personal opinion is the same.

So we know that James Durden features in the first picture, but who is the lady? There are no clues at all here. Moving names into the frame turned out to be a fruitless exercise. Both Webster and Durden had wives and sisters. Webster's sister, Gertrude, features on the 1901 census as living in the Chelverton House and is described as a governess. It looks as if she moved into the Broomville Rd property after Webster married Susan and the Webster family set up house together. James was the youngest of his three siblings, but it seems unlikely that his elder sister Edith would have been presented in this way. Maybe it was a picture of a younger Ruby round about the time of their engagement or wedding but it simply doesn't look like her and anyway why is it not separately framed to form a matching pair? I can't find a picture of Susan Webster but it's really stretching the realms of possibility to think that a portrait of Webster's wife would appear in this context.

Another theory could suggest that like this was a commission carried out by Webster. This theory is rather destroyed by the obvious conclusion that if this is the case, the painting never reached its destination. Was it a commission that was rejected (surely not) or no longer required?

Maybe it's the result of a simple accident of convenience sometimes seen in the art world. Did Webster simply run out of canvas or frame space and utilise the equipment and materials he had on hand at the time Perhaps he intended to reframe the second portrait later and then never did. Maybe the mystery lady has nothing to do with either Webster or Durden?

The fact remains that the painting on display in the frame is Durden and the painting behind has always has always been known by the family as a mystery subject. It's very tempting to assume that because the paintings appear to be a pair then the lady must be connected to Durden in some way.

So the mystery remains! We will never know why this portrait appears to be hidden behind the Webster portrait of his friend James Durden. More importantly, we will also probably never know the identity of this young lady.

Interestingly there is another portrait of James painted by W E Webster. This is owned by Janet. Comparing this picture with the first portrait would suggest that it was painted round about the same time. The face is presented in profile with the same receding hairline and distinctive features. There may be a slight time gap between the pictures, but James does look about the same age on both of them. The suggestion of similarity between the two pictures is supported by the clothes worn by James on each occasion.The copy I have of this second portrait is in colour, so it helps suggest the colours that may have featured in the first black and white picture. The suit is of a heavy textured material in grey with a matching waistcoat and the tie is red. Again there is a high white collar. This portrait extends further than the head and shoulders and one hand is showing as it emerges from the white cuff of the right hand sleeve to rest gently on the lap. On this occasion James is seated as the outline of the high back dark chair appears behind his right shoulder. There is no second portrait behind this painting.

Given that both pictures are owned by the family it seems possible to suggest that maybe Ruby or Betty asked their friend Walter Webster to paint the pictures of her husband and or father

Whatever the provenance of these two striking portraits of James, the mystery about the lost or forgotten picture, hidden behind the first portrait remains. It's an intriguing artistic conundrum and at the time of writing neither the family nor I have any idea about the identity of this young lady or why she was hidden from view. It's a mystery.

.

Sunshine and Shadow

Derwentwater

16: A Sense of Place

Durden is known as a landscape artist as well as a portrait painter and some of his pictures reflect life around him. The ability to tell a story is always there. As representatives of his work I have chosen five examples, some of which have not been seen in the public arena before. They also show his ability to use different media. *June Morning, Country Auction* and *Grasmere Sports* are all in oils but the Aladin paintings are watercolours and the Millbeck farms are pencil sketches.

June Morning features a young lady, seated at a circular table positioned by an open French Window with a city-scape beyond. The colours are muted, but the narrative is established immediately. She is reading a letter and the viewer is drawn into the story. Refreshment is forgotten as she absorbs the contents. The familiar characteristics of a Durden are there . . . flowers, including blue delphiniums and the drop of the turquoise curtain.

Another of his paintings features a 'prop' used in the June Morning picture. A *Country Auction* presents the sale of the contents of a country house or estate and one of the items is recognisably the white chair from round the table. The auction is attended by a crowd of interested spectators, the suggestion of serious bidding, and a jolly gathering of folk having an entertaining day out. The auctioneer is in full flow, raising his arm to acknowledge a bid and a gold framed picture is being carried away by his assistants. However the focus of this picture appears to be the figure in the left hand corner of the painting. This is an elderly gentleman standing away from the crowds in the shelter of a tree. He has removed his hat from his balding head and in his other hand he holds a handkerchief to his slightly

159

June Morning
Keswick Museum and Art Gallery

bowed face. At its simplest level, the implication is that here is the heart-broken owner of the estate witnessing the breakup of his home. Another figure, hardly seen, is partially concealed by a neighbouring tree. This is an elderly lady in dark clothing with a black hat and gloves and this adds to the narrative of this sad aged couple losing their family home and its contents. A second old lady, also in black is seated and there is a suggestion of a conversation taking place. Further examination shows a young lady, clad in brown shorts and a short-sleeved cream shirt. She is leaning against the tree trunk.She looks relaxed, but her face is turned away from the artist. She is regarding the crowd and the viewer is left to decide what expression her face would be showing. To my mind, she presents a meloncholy figure. The head of a young man standing next to her leads to the conjecture that maybe he is connected to her. Again, a narrative could be constructed around these figures and I spent some time deciding that this could be a family, the heart-broken man with his wife and possibly mother or sister and then daughter and son-in-law. The figures in the shadows are so mixed in with the auction lots and the seated older lady in black is virtually indistinguishable. As a final point, the use of light emphasises a narrative. The cheerful crowd of onlookers in casual colourful dress with white shirts and sun hats are in full sunlight on this lovely day, but our tragic gentleman and his family are in the darker shade of the tree and untouched by any sunshine both physically and metaphorically. I have to add that conjecture about the story is, of course, a personal opinion.

Durden was a quiet and unassuming man and I suspect that one of the attractions of living in Millbeck was the opportunity to get on with his life and paintings without the need for much involvement in social contacts. The village was sparsely populated and quiet and farming folk around him would also wish to get on with the day to day routine in a fairly taciturn Cumbrian way. No doubt pleasantries were exchanged as milk was delivered or collected and the post van arrived, but basically the family were at liberty to join in with the traditional pursuits or not. These were based on the seasons of the farming year with

Country Auction

such events as Christmas and Harvest dictating social interaction. I suspect he came across as rather a diffident chap, regarded as an offcomer and an artist, but accepted with respect and affection within the village community.

By 1937 both Betty and Joe had left home. James and Ruby had a day out at the annual Grasmere sports. This had its origins in the mid-nineteenth century as the annual Grasmere Sheep Fair, initially held on the first Tuesday in September. It quickly developed into a social occasion attended by the farming communities with farm hands, stone wallers and shepherds. The competitive element amongst these young men soon led to a variety of sports. It is now known as Lakeland Sports and the Show, held at Grasmere has been there annually since 1868, with breaks for the two world wars. The traditional Cumberland and Westmorland wrestling was an established favourite with the competitors wearing the time honoured costumes of white leggings, dark shorts and white vest tops. Prestigious status, prizes and medals were given to the winners. Fell racing developed with the initial route up to the 1200 ft top of Butter

Grasmere Sports

Crags, round the flag and down again to the sports field. Another Guides Race went to the top of Silver Howe at one stage. Hound trailing followed the same sort of routes and sheepdog trials took place. The whole show is now a significant and very popular Lakeland attraction taking place at the end of August, featuring all the customary and historic activities along with traditional stalls and refreshments and all the trappings of a country fair.

Durden depicted this event in an oil painting in 1937. He chose his vantage point as part way up the grassy fell shown in the foreground left hand corner of the picture, so had an extensive aerial view of the sports field and the surrounding area. Below him sits the oval field as the focal point of the activities and this space is surrounded by spectators depicting the usual crowds on this important day out. Transport is parked on the outskirts of the crowd. Cars are shown in the fields beyond either side of the old road, but in the foreground the bright colours of the charabancs catch the eye. Two are red and two a striking yellow, with various others not quite as colourful in evidence. The sports arena has a couple of isolated events taking place, possibly two bouts of wrestling and a platform or podium is shown at the edge of the arena. The lake features in the middle distance to the right of the landscape, with trees and fells rising steeply behind. This stunning rural scene is completed by the appearance, on the far left, of the houses at the edge of the village with the square church tower showing through the trees. Durden appears to have adopted exactly the right perspective and viewpoint to capture and present this age old unchanging panorama with a delightful contrast between the peace and tranquillity of rural Lakeland and the bustle and excitement of this traditional event.

Two years earlier in 1935 Durden used another artistic medium to produce a delightful pencil sketch of a farm in Millbeck. Low Grove Farm, situated just along the road below Millbeck Place was one of the oldest settlements in the parish. The barns are thought to be from the sixteenth century and the date on the lintel above the front door of the farmhouse is 1746. It was occupied in 1829 by Joseph Dover, the nephew of Daniel Dover who was living in Skiddaw Bank and these two men eventually controlled the woollen industry in Millbeck. Its probable that woollen cloth was dried on the terraces. In 1897 the property was purchased by Samuel Brownrigg, but the family were only in residence at Low Grove for a year before buying Millbeck Hall estate.

Later, William Thompson became the tenant. Quite a character within the community, he was affectionately known as 'Butty' and was a contemporary of the Durden family. He wasn't averse to a bit of a 'crack' when out and about and I would guess he and Durden would exchange pleasantries if Durden was taking a stroll along the top road.

On a personal level the Thompson family were still in residence when we came to Applethwaite. Whilst I was out one day walking our border collie we were joined by one of the farm dogs, who often came with us if on the loose and pottering about the yard. Butty came along in his battered farm vehicle, wound the window down for a bit of a crack. During the chat about the weather he looked at the dog and said, '"Eh I've got yan that looks just like that!"

Like most of the village Durden ignored the title of Low Grove and his sketch is labelled Thompson's Farm and dated September 8th 1935. This hitherto unseen drawing came out of

Durden's sketchbook and may have been a preparatory exercise for a planned painting, but as yet I have found no evidence. Like the Grasmere sports picture, the perspective is shown from above and must have been sketched from the road. This ribbon development is known as the terrace road and anyone on that road looks down on the back of the farm. The front of the handsome double fronted farmhouse with its stout old front door faces down its own access road as it runs down to the Carlisle road below. Durden's sketch therefore features the back view of the farm and barns and outbuildings. It shows the gable end of part of the farmhouse on the right hand side with the gate through to the yard and barns on the left. The pencil detail on the barns shows how different building materials have been used over the centuries, but the farmhouse looks unchanged with the same architectural features as today. The trees are still in late summer foliage, but the fields are bare as obviously harvest is complete. A single hay stook shows up in one field just below the barns. It's a delightful little cameo and captures the peace and perspective of this Lakeland farm sitting comfortably in the landscape where it was born.

    In the same sketch book there is another pencil sketch of a farm and again there seems to be no evidence of this ever developing into a painting that I can trace. This is of Applethwaite Farm and is dated some weeks previously on the 25th of August 1935. Again the viewpoint is almost aerial with Durden apparently standing on the terrace road or in the fields above the farm and looking down at the buildings. The pencil detail is intricate and comprehensive. The sketch is dominated by a large tree behind the barns and the view of the farm is mostly sloping barn rooves. The farmhouse is one of the oldest buildings in the village. It is often the chosen scene for art groups painting and sketching outside in the summer. Had Durden opted to paint this traditional view of the front of this attractive whitewashed building, he would have been able to include its main feature, the front door. This original metal studded, cross boarded oak front door dates back to earlier turbulent time highlighting the area's relative proximity to the Scottish Border. It's a formidable,

The Post Gets Through

interesting architectural hallmark and would have provided a significant level of security for the farm. I'd love to ask Durden why he decided to sketch the barn rooves from the back instead of the picturesque front aspect!

A final picture of the village landscape is an undated painting which shows the village under a heavy snowfall. The view point is from Millbeck Place down the path through the garden towards Lake View Farm. Snow blankets the hedges alongside the garden path and the field and buildings are also white over. The dark green evergreen hedge and a tall fir tree provide some colour in the foreground, but this is not a crisp winter day with a blue sky and icing sugar silhouettes of frosty fells. Rather it is a more typical winter's day and the morning looks grey, cold and hugely uninviting. The distant fells are just visible, but they disappear into a bleak horizon where only the suggestion of shadows and snow give any impression of distance and perspective. Some bare brown trees show up in the middle distance, but it is a bleak impression of days so familiar to those of us living in this area.

However the painting boasts one striking cheery focal point and the whole painting and feeling of the day is lifted. Round the corner behind the tall green conifer comes the post van. It's still partly behind the tree, but its blob of vivid post office red immediately shines out on this dreary colourless day. Durden calls this picture *The Post Gets Through* and the simplicity of this title leads to all sorts of other responses. Suddenly there is contact with outside world. The village is no longer cut off or sitting in snowy isolation . With the arrival of the post van comes anticipation of deliveries and human contact as the postman tramps up snowy paths and tracks to push all variety of correspondence into farms and cottages. The title also gives the impression that it has been a struggle to manoeuvre the red van through roads out of Keswick and up blocked lanes to the centre of the of Millbeck. I so wish this painting was dated .... surely it has to be a December time with the thoughts of Christmas cards and letters. I love this painting. Initially it could be described as drab and depressing, but the suggested movement of this one red van changes everything and with one brush stroke Durden introduces some optimism to the day.

I'm using four rather more quirky landscapes as representative of Durden's undoubted talent as a stage designer. In this case they really are exactly that . . . scenery designs for a dramatic production. These four are previously unseen, although they were on show in Christmas 1918 when they featured as backdrops to the Grand Xmas Pantomime of Aladdin and his Lamp. At the time Durden was serving in the First World War and, like many of the troops in difficult circumstances, these soldiers created their own entertainment. It's amazing how much could be produced from so little and how an irrepressible sense of humour could surface often with hilarious results in the middle of a war.

This particular performance is sub-titled as A Pantomime in two Acts and Eight Gas Attacks and the programme credits show *The whole of the Scenery painted by Pte Durden A.O.C.*

The detailed water colours, painted on pieces of card 9 x 5½ inches depict how the story moves along and two of them show the faint pencil squares where presumably the design was copied and transferred to the back drop. There were five scenes in Act one. Scene one was the Demons' Cave and a spectacular mountainous rocky area illustrates this setting. A massive rock boulder dominates the scene and to the right, the mouth of the receding cave disappears into an ominous black hole. It contrasts hugely with the predominant colours of grey and blue around the entrance and the audiences eye is drawn into this space. I love the fact that Durden couldn't resist adding the rather attractive detail of a self seeded sapling springing up on a rocky ledge at

167

the other side of the cave. The roots are clinging onto the precipitous cliff edge, but the tree still produces some red berries which add to the contrast of the black hole of the cave beneath. All those practice exercises sketching trees and intricate details of foliage in London parks for exam submissions really paid off!

There must have been a very hasty scene change as the action moved immediately to Scene 2 in China Town. This is a beautiful little cameo water colour in its own right with the characteristic Durden use of light, shadow and colours. The vivid blue sky is broken by the rooves of two pagodas with their triangular shapes. Further buildings show up behind with a row of shops opposite, some with items spilling onto a wide street, which sweeps away and round a corner into a distant perspective. The shadow of the shops is outlined on the pavement below. Flowers abound with typical blue and orange pink suggestions of profusion (careful James . . . it's beginning to look like an English summer garden!) The focal point is a Chinese figure in the middle distance. He is wearing the traditional single cobalt blue tunic with matching trousers and conical-shaped hat. His attention is directed at the forefront of the smaller pagoda where there is a suggestion of figures in the interior of the low balcony area. Other figures are shown on the other side of the road where two or three are leaning over an outside shop perimeter fence next to a barrel to chat to a figure off the scene. However these figures are rather obscure as they stand within the shadow of the building. Interestingly the pencil squares to facilitate the transfer of plan to back drop show up very clearly on this delightful water colour and closer examination reveals a further tall pagoda sketched in pencil on the blue horizon. The suggestion of a work in progress is fascinating!

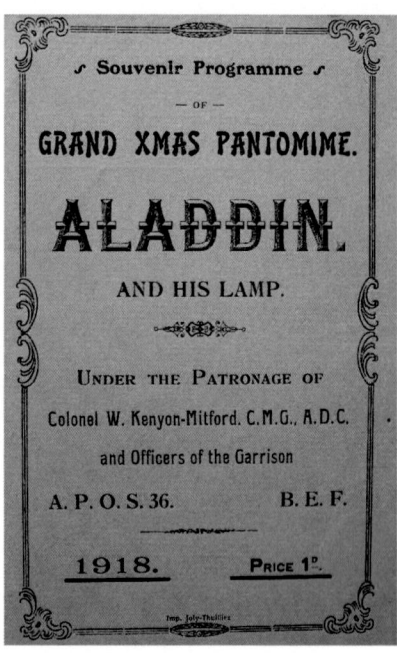

Souvenir Programme

— OF —

GRAND XMAS PANTOMIME.

ALADDIN.

AND HIS LAMP.

UNDER THE PATRONAGE OF

Colonel W. Kenyon-Mitford. C.M.G., A.D.C.

and Officers of the Garrison

A. P. O. S. 36.   B. E. F.

1918.   PRICE 1ᴰ.

Imp. July-Thuillier

The pantomime moves on and scene three takes the audience On the Way to the Cave. I wonder if the backdrop for scene one was deployed again?

Next comes scene four and the Interior of the cave. Here the fearful black depths are revealed with rocks in the foreground and the suggestion of stalactites at the back of the cave. However the middle of the cave tells a different story where a string of what look like fairy lights dip down in an arc to throw a surprising amount of illumination onto the floor of the cave. The edge of one rock is lit up up in shades of pink, cream and orange sandstone. Nestling in its shelter there is a multicoloured collection of treasures beneath. They are rather indistinguishable (Is one a gold lamp?) but presumably the props department had fun scrounging such treasures from the supplies depot. Aladdin's Cave indeed!

Scene five is the interior of Widow Twankey's Laundry. There are only three scenes in Act 2, China Town, The Public Baths and finally Chrysanthemum Land. Only one design survives and it looks as if Durden thoroughly enjoyed himself producing a spectacular English Garden scene where a profusion of chrysanthemums run riot. A broken slate pathway leads the eye to two tall stone columns. Beyond the pillars the viewers are taken to to the distant horizon of a brilliant cobalt blue sky and a distant fell, which would do justice to anything in a Lake District panorama on a summer's day. Orange, yellow and pink flowers

169

dominate the design and in typical Durden style, light and shadow is used to emphasise the columns and vivid blue sky. Dark green trees in the top corners frame the scene.

Before we leave this section of Durden's work it's worth a slightly more detailed look at the programme itself. The cast is listed under the careful mis-spelling of cast and features the IMMORTALS and the MORTALS . Each character is given further advice as to the presentation of their role. So the Demon King is *as played by Charlie Chaplin at Brewery Lane* and his opposite number *The Fairy Queen as played by Marie Lloyd at the Electric Theatre, Brixton* Within the mortals Aladdin has a simple instruction as played by Dr Crippen,. Widow Twankey *As played by Pimple in 'Should A Woman Tell?'* Abanaza in *The wicked Uncle assisted by his little dog Candie in 'The Ladies Delight.' Princess So-Shi is as played by Wilkie Bard*. The Emperor has no advice but is simply described as *He of the thin legs and no ambition* and finally the two Policemen are Authors of the famous story 'Hold my lamp Aladdin'.

This looks like an attempt at a professional production; it has a Musical Director, a Business Manager, a Prompter and an Electrician. The posters have been designed and executed by a lieutenant with *Costumes and Wigs by Willie Clarkson, London*. 'Oriental Lanterns are made by the 37th Company C. L.C. by kind permission of Capt Joachim and the whole pantomime is supported by the Chorus of the Men of the Garrison. Within the context of its time it must have been hilarious and undoubtedly a triumph!

In some ways the most entertaining section of this programme is the back page where several pieces of guidance, advice and even instructions are delivered to the audience. It would certainly give then something to think about before the performance or during the interval. One wonders if the first statement was the suggestion of Durden as it reads: *The Audience is requested not to take the scenery away.*

Audience safety is obviously a priority as this is followed by: *In case of an air raid the Audience are requested to lie perfectly still until carried to a place of safety by the performers* As well as: *The Audience will be medically examined after each performance.* Helpful concessions are delivered: *Orderly Sergts, P.B. Men, Batmen, Cooks and other irritations admitted half price to the boxes. Plus Seats may be booked at the Cookhouse, Garrison Hospital.*

Apparently the Incidental Music and Lighting effects are by "TICKLER" and "MACHONACHIE" and finally after an evening of pantomime jollity, the audience is reassured that *Ambulances and G.S. Waggons will arrive at 10pm.*

The price for this souvenir programme was one penny. Duren must have spent quite a lot of time designing the scenery and he then executed the backdrops. It has a 'such larks old chap' feeling about it and I love the fact that this programme, such a small piece of now very yellowing paper survived. It's a stunning example of historical ephemera that could so easily have been lost. I suppose we've all kept souvenir programmes as just that . . . a souvenir and a memory of a happy evening, a memorable stage production or individual performance. I love to think that Durden kept it to remind him of his contribution to that merry Christmas evening and think about everyone involved.

17: Rabbit Holes!

There are a lot of loose ends in the Durden story and inevitably these can lead to rabbit hole expeditions. However some of them proved fascinating in their connections with the Durden narrative. So whilst many of these loose ends will remain unresolved, it is possible to bring some of them together. This book never set out to be a complete biography and I apologise for not doing justice to Janet Durden-Hey's magnificent archive. Her generosity in sharing so much information on her grandfather meant that various interested parties were able to access significant and previously unknown stories about this artist. With the help of volunteer Pamela Herbert, Keswick Museum was subsequently able to digitise all the archive material and it is now available as a research facility. Durden's local museum can pride itself on being the major source for his biographical material and it owes a huge debt of gratitude to the Durden-Hey family.

  I became very interested in the the senior Ellis family and of course without the injection of funding from them it's doubtful that Durden would have had the opportunities to make his way as quickly and successfully as he did. Joseph Ellis devoted much of his time, self-taught expertise and increasing experience to the development of the iron and steel industry on the West coast of Cumberland. After a brief time in Claygate in Surrey, the family returned to the north. From Lorne Villas in Workington, they took up residence in Ingwell Hall, a magnificent detached house on Moor Row, outside Whitehaven. The impressive portico of the front door boasts Grecian columns which are easily recognisable on some of the photographs of the Ellis family. One shows Sarah Martha Ellis standing outside this portico accompanied by a small dog and another features the house from a distance with an impressive array of what look like daffodils.

In 1920 Joseph Ellis retired and the family chose to spend their retirement in Keswick. They rented Skiddaw Lodge, on Vicarage Hill, from Sir John Randles. The Randles were living next door in Bristowe Hill, a superb Edwardian House on the edge of Keswick. Occupying a prime site on a small hill, it was built for Sir John and Lady Randles in 1903. Hodgsons, the Keswick builders, have a detailed account book showing itemised costs including transport of slate from Honister Slate mine by the cartload operated by one man and his donkey.

Born in Boston, Lincolnshire in 1857, the son of a Wesleyan minister, John Scurragh Randles, was also instrumental in the development of the iron and steel industry in West Cumberland. His social and business relationship with the Ellis family was a significant factor in the growth of this powerful industry. He was also a Member of Parliament, initially representing Cockermouth and later Northwest Manchester. He was knighted in 1905 for his public services. He had the interests of his home area at heart and is remembered in Keswick as a generous benefactor, giving time, energy and finance to various projects. He gave land to the National Trust and supported the Wesleyan Methodist Church in Southey Street. His wife, the former Elizabeth Harley, spent many years on the Ladies Committee of the Mary Hewetson Cottage Hospital working tirelessly for the benefit of this institution. This was recognised when a new operating theatre was opened. George Bott in his 'Brief History 1892- 1992 of The Mary Hewetson Cottage Hospital Keswick' says: *The new operating theatre was lavishly equipped and justly claimed to be the most up to date in the county, possibly the country. The sterilising room was the first of its kind in Britain and the fittings in the theatre itself had been specially made to the most modern standards and style using stainless steel wherever possible. The only timber in the building was that used for oak doors.*

The plaque above the entrance reads: *The Lady Randles Theatre, presented by Sir John S. Randles in recognition of his wife's great interest in the welfare of the Hospital. 2nd June 1932.*

There is another plaque at the Cottage Hospital and it almost looks as if Joseph Ellis followed the example of his friend. A separate unit at the back of the hospital now houses the Physiotherapy department and an adjoining stone built lodge bears a slate plaque which reads: *MEMORIAL LODGE / presented by / JOSEPH ELLIS / IN MEMORY OF HIS WIFE / SARAH MARTHA ELLIS / HIS SON / JAMES VALENTINE ELLIS / HIS DAUGHTER / LILIAN MARY ELLIS*

No dates are given on the plaque, but in 1936 it is recorded that a bequest from the Ellis family covered most of the funding for a caretaker's lodge and a children's ward. This would make absolute sense chronologically as James Valentine Ellis (Ruby's brother) died in 1935 and Lily (Ruby's sister) died in 1936. Within 2 years Joseph lost a son and a daughter, in what must have been a tragic loss for the 86 year old.

Living in Millbeck, Ruby was now near enough to keep an eye on her elderly parents and be on hand when Sarah Martha died in 1925. It would appear that Joseph continued to live at Skiddaw Lodge until 1936 when the house was purchased by the Sarsfield-Hall family. Joseph died, aged 90, in 1940 at 'Brockleside' the home of his son Wilfred Ellis, with whom he lived for the last three years of his life . His obituary in the Keswick Reminder on February 9th 1940, is surprisingly brief, but it acknowledges his significant contribution to the iron and steel industry and I quote: *Mr Ellis was the first managing director of the Workington Hematite Iron and Steel Co. Ltd and Sir John Randles was chairman of the directors and it was through that company that the two men built up the iron and steel industry of West Cumberland through the rationalisation of the industry so that the Co. owned its own iron ore mines,*

Joseph Ellis

coal mines coke ovens and became a self sufficient unit of industry. Mr Ellis retained his connection with the Co. Until 1920 when it was taken over by the United Steel Company.

    A later undated photograph shows the children with their grandparents on seats at the edge of a grass tennis court. The children look older here, maybe in the region of 10 and 12 years old, but it's difficult to estimate. Grandmother Sarah Martha, and Grandfather Joseph are easily identifiable relaxing in garden chairs. Sarah is reading a book. Young Joe is sitting cross legged on the grass at the foot of a deck chair and it looks as if the occupant is his mother Ruby, but unfortunately her face is obscured by a sun hat. Betty leans on the back of this same chair. The group is completed by James, but again the poor quality of the photograph makes it difficult to be sure of his identity. It looks as if he may be lighting a pipe, which would make sense as we know he is a pipe-smoker. The foliage and flowers in the background would suggest it's summer and it's a lovely gentle picture of a family relaxing in the sunshine by the tennis court. This might well be Ingwell? It's too early for Skiddaw Lodge or Skiddaw Bank.

    Another loose end which deserves some attention, focuses on the Durden family and the early background of James. As this was never intended to be a chronological biography and I knew when James was born, it was quite some time through the project before I sent for his birth certificate. I had assumed that it wouldn't tell me much more than I already knew and in some ways this proved to be the case. The birth certificate confirmed that James was born on the 29th November, 1877, to James and Mary Ellen (formerly Swarbrick) and that his father James was a maker up of cotton goods. The birth was registered on 28th December 1877. The interesting information here was the address, 17, March Street. A map of the time identifies this as one of a series of streets within central Manchester in the area of the Royal Infirmary. The streets were named after months of the year starting with January Street and running in parallel rows through to July Street. Logically March Street is the third street down branching off from Upper Brook Street.

175

The Ordnance Survey map of 1888-1913 shows these streets as rows of terraced houses in the back to back style developed to accommodate the workers of the industrial revolution. They were thrown up quite quickly as the working population shifted from a rural environment to the cities, to feed the woollen and cotton mills and keep the wheels of the Industrial Revolution turning. Canals and railways also developed at speed and Manchester became the power-house of the North. James was born into this smoke-filled world of factory chimneys, dirty and congested streets, gas lights and clattering trams. The whole area can be seen on the map running southwest of Upper Brook Street in the direction of the Royal Infirmary, with March Street situated at right angles to Upper Brook Street. The Christie Hospital, with the word 'cancer' identified in brackets and the Royal Eye Hospital are marked on the map. March Street backed onto York Place and thence through to the main thoroughfare of Oxford Road. Interestingly enough Plymouth Grove is also within this area and number 84 was the home of Elizabeth Gaskell the writer, who lived there with her minister husband William from 1850-1865. The Vicarage is of course rather a grand Georgian building, but Gaskell is renowned for her humanitarian approach to mill workers living in considerably less acceptable accommodation around her. She was involved in the area on several levels. Her monumental novel *North and South* describes the environment of the satanic mills of the North in vivid and striking detail and she is living only streets away from Durden's birthplace. Admittedly there is a time gap of 12 years and whilst the environment may have improved, the physical features of houses and streets are still the same and this is where James was born.

 A modern map shows a very different picture. March Street has long since gone probably during the urban (slum) clearance programme of the 1960's or possibly even earlier during the punitive bombing raids of the Second World War. The whole area has now been developed with extensions to the Royal Infirmary and the growth of the University quarter.

 I can't resist throwing in a very personal connection to a loose end here. My parents, newly married in 1939, were living in Cheadle Hume during the war. My father was a draughtsman and mechanical engineer in a Reserved Occupation involved with bridge design. He also worked with the Auxillery Fire Service at nights during the bombing raids. Like many men with dangerous and distressing wartime experiences, he never talked about this in later life and his uniform and peaked hat plus badge hung in the attic for many years. My mother vividly recalls emerging from the neighbour's Anderson shelter at dawn during the worst of those years and watching desperately for him to turn the corner at the end of their street and come home. In a total flight of fancy I wonder if he ever put foot in March Street!

The Durden family were still in March Street in 1881 and the census return records father James at 32 as a 'maker up of clothes', his wife Mary E also 32 and the children Edith 6, Alfred 5 and James 3. However by 1891 the family have moved a few hundred yards northwards up the road and just round the corner. They are now in Granville Street at Number 15 and appear to be going up in the world a little. A postcard of Granville Steet in 1911 shows a wide cobbled street still with terrace houses, but with bay windows and quite a spacious aspect for an industrial environment. Unfortunately the occupation of James senior is rather obscured by an indistinct scribble right over the top of the entry, but it looks as if it might read 'Manager in Pack House'. This too seems to indicate some progress in the workplace from the factory floor to a managerial position? Edith at 17, is a dressmaker and Alfred has found employment as a clerk . The 13 year old James is described as a scholar and we know by the age of 16 he is producing the beautiful bird paintings referred to in the first chapter.

Space prohibits me describing Durden's flower pictures but he obviously made full use of the Millbeck garden. His blue delphiniums often feature and he loved the yellow dasies. Janet recalls him picking one and wearing it in his button-hole on summer mornings. There is also a striking painting of orange and yellow poppies.

One particular rabbit hole I couldn't resist peering down was one provided by a black and white photograph of a portrait and

177

two apparently unfinished letters. I'm sure the letters were finished, but the last pages appear to have gone astray. These were with a photograph of a portrait of a dignified mature couple seated either side of a white fireplace in a rather grand and opulent sitting room. The photograph was taken by a W. H. Grove, 73 Earls Court Road, Kensington, but there were no names on the back. However the content of the letters indicated clearly that the portrait and the letters referred to the same subject.

The lady is dark haired, slim and elegant. She is wearing a long afternoon dress and a pleasant smile. She appears engaging and graceful. She is in charge of a small table upon which rests a tray with a teapot and a silver Georgian coffee pot with appropriate accompaniments. The gentleman opposite her is presumably her husband and he is relaxing in a low backed armless chair with an open book in his hand. He has obviously finished reading the newspaper which is discarded half open, by the side of his chair. Above the white (marble?) fireplace is an large rectangular ornately framed mirror. It reflects the opposite wall where two other portraits are mounted. They show pictures of two young men, or possibly one young man and a lady? To the left of the seated gentleman is a glass door giving a limited view of part of what was probably an extensive garden. A lawn runs down to foliage and trees and there is a suggestion of a circular flower bed or even a fountain on the lawn. Certainly a small ornamental figure can be seen in the middle of the circle.

The first letter connected to this portrait is sent to James Durden on the 15th of October, 1938. The headed notepaper is marked Craignahullie, Skelmorlie. The letter is unfinished and unsigned, but it soon becomes obvious that the correspondence is from the lady who features in the portrait. She is returning a rough sketch and is impressed with Durden, complimenting him that *after so few sights of our faces you've got such obvious likenesses is little short of amazing*. She jokes that she likes the dress he's given her and says that some day she will *beg the sketch back again to take to my dressmaker as a fashion plate*.

She draws him a diagram of the long wall in the drawing room labelling a square as "a big Robert Houston picture" (50x40 inches) in place and a suggestion where the new portrait would be hung.

There is some discussion and suggestions about where the couple will pose when they sit for the actual portrait ... maybe a couch by the fire or different chairs that can be moved. She tells Durden her housekeeper had seen the sketch and exclaimed *that's just the way you sit* but she further comments *it certainly isn't when I'm doing a crossword puzzle*. However she recognises that all the details of furniture, shifting the mirror ... can be worked out when you come. You'll have to paint the mirror much larger than it really is to put both boys in!

She moves to the logistics of Durden's appointment. She says the extension to the rock garden will soon be finished, but on the 23rd she is invited to visit Sir Oliver Lodge and doesn't like to say "some other time" to him. She eventually suggests Tuesday 1st November ... and here the letter tails off with no further pages available!

It looks as if this date was acceptable to our artist as the next letter is dated 11th June 1939 and the project is complete. Not only has the picture been finished, but the writer now reports: *This morning the picture has been hung, on the inner wall of the dining room, ... it looks lovely there! The Stuart Browns lunched with us and asked at once if we will loan it to the Paisley Show*

179

this autumn. Answer in the affirmative.

This is a friendly and sociable letter describing the couples' recent trip South. They have been in the Lake District as she gives details of them motoring from garden to garden and Grasmere, Seascale, Wrynose and Hardknott are mentioned although the latter was avoided in the end. She reports that Jim has a scalded arm and strained knee thanks to Wrynose so maybe the car has failed on this pass? They've had good weather as she comments that they are very very brown Browns and seems to delight in the pun. One wonders if they collected the finished portrait on this trip? She asks for the account for this conversation piece and then observes rather charmingly *altho we don't seem to be saying much to each other - however that's a sign of long happy years of thoughts shared!* She seems to think Durden will be off to the States soon and jokes *where the temptations are many, so be business-like for once!*

She is excited about their next adventure, as Jim has been asked to go on a business trip to Australia and New Zealand and she points out his devoted wife can't be left behind. She has magnificent plans for travels after the business is completed and lists *The Great Barrier Reef, New Guinea, Java, Singapore, Borneo, Hong Kong, Japan, The Philippines, San Francisco (and my sister) and if I can wangle it a few more.* She adds: *Perhaps we'll meet at Zuni, New Mexico, and you'll give me a painting lesson? Grand stuff, there!* Three more lines at the bottom of the page of this last sheet say: *Tell Joe that his godson is John all over again, in looks and happy nature, a beautiful boy.*

So is this the conclusion to the letter? If it is, she has left herself no space to sign off (and give me her identity). To my immense relief she has scribbled the farewell in the margin of the first page and I find: *With regards to you all and many thanks for the art treasure achieved under such difficulties, I am ever sincerely yours, Lucia S. Brown.*

No indication about what the difficulties were but maybe the date of June 1939 is significant, three months before the outbreak of World War II. Mercifully, the letters were written in quite a legible script on headed notepaper and the address was given as

Craignahullie, Skelmorlie. So with a name, an address and a sister in San Francisco, the story was fairly easy to follow up.

Lucia Brown was an American, the daughter of Charles Seeberger who invented the escalator. She married James Hally Brown and the couple moved into Craignahullie in Skelmorlie in Scotland, round about 1917. James or Jim was a Brown of Brown and Polsons, the Paisley firm of cornflour and starch manufacturers. They lived in Craignahullie for over fifty years, from 1917 until 1969. The history of the house is covered in some detail in Fifty Years of Skelmorlie Community Centre 1948 - 1998 by Eddie Scott. The house itself has a fascinating past with some interesting occupants, but all that really is a rabbit hole too far!

The reference in the October 1938 letter to making the mirror much larger in the portrait so it can accommodate the reflection of the portraits of the two boys is interesting as at some point in 1938 there was a family death. John Brown, the 28 year old son, died from blood poisoning. Perhaps this accident took place after the letter was written, so between October and the end of December, as there is no mention of John's death. Maybe Durden already knew about it or maybe the topic is too painful to mention. Further tragedy awaited the family when Charles, another son died in 1941. Charles was a pilot with the RAF, flying with 101 Squadron and his plane was shot down off the French coast at Boulogne. He was 26 and his name is recorded on the Skelmorlie and Wemyss Bay War Memorial. His parents bought a house called Stroove in the village with the intention of setting it up as a cottage hospital as a memorial to their two sons. A trust fund was set up for the conversion and maintenance of the building, but after some difficulties with health service administrators, the cottage became a community centre instead. In time this was rebuilt as a library and community centre and was a valuable asset to the village.

The Browns continued to live at Craignahullie for the rest of their lives,celebrating their Golden Wedding there in March 1957. They continued supporting the village and community in many generous ways and were acknowledged as significant

181

benefactors. Lucia Brown was an interesting character and the villagers were used to seeing her collecting sheep's wool from hedgerows and fences, which she took home and spun into yarn. It was dyed with natural dyes and turned into tweed cloth for her husband's suits. She was also a member of the Royal Asiatic Society for Great Britain and Ireland and became Vice President of the Scottish Rock Garden Club in 1954. She died in December 1968, a year after the death of her husband in February 1967.

So apologies for some of this seemingly trivial detail in this penultimate chapter, but rabbit holes are sometimes made irresistible because of the people and the characters that occupy them Once you have a place name and location or more importantly a face and a name, stories must be told!

Mixed Bunch, Flowers in a Vase
Keswick Museum and Art Gallery

18: Rest in Peace

Life at Millbeck Place changed dramatically and tragically for James in the Spring of 1958, when Ruby died in the famly home on the 21st April. The cause of death on the death certificate is given as massive pulmonary embolism and thrombosis of Iliac vein. No time then to call an ambulance or take her to the Cottage Hospital so generously supported by her father. The death is registered on the 26th of April by Betty.

Betty and Leonard subsequently moved from London to Millbeck and life must have brightened up a little with the extended visit of his granddaughter, Janet, Joe's daughter. With the family living in America, James hadn't seen much of her since she was a little girl.

There is a really delightful photograph of James with this granddaughter down by the lake taken round about 1951, when Joe and Kathleen were visiting Millbeck. James is sitting at the water's edge wearing a Panama hat and with the customary cigarette in his hand. Janet, aged 7, is pottering peacefully, but purposefully, on the stony shore next to him. She is taking care not to hurt her bare feet on the stones and holds out one arm to balance her rather precarious movements. The background of a calm lake and an island complete this lovely picture and to me it captures the casual appeal of the endless sunny summer days of a childhood playing by the lake. (The irresistible appeal of Swallows and Amazons comes to mind and I have a similar photograph of my own daughter playing in almost the identical place). There is also an equally interesting photograph which looks as if it was taken the same day, of James, Kathleen and Janet perched on a rocky outcrop on the lake shore (at a guess it could be in the region of Friars Crag?) Janet thinks it was taken on one of the islands. The background is clearly Skiddaw.

By the time Janet reappears after Ruby's death, she is 16 and this time she spends a year in Millbeck Place. She and James get to know each other again and obviously enjoy each other's company. James describes her in a letter as *a tough little lass . . . she seems to tackle anything that comes along*. With much affection he called her 'Copper Knob' and his 'Lass from Lancashire'. Janet has many happy memories of that period, particularly his pleasure in taking tea on the terrace whatever the weather and eating his favourite seed cake. In fact Janet recalls learning to make that cake. She remembers him peeling potatoes in freezing cold water with hands that were blue with cold. His smoking habit didn't change but the pipe of his student days was replaced with cigarettes. This was greeted with huge disapproval from Betty and he would retreat from her criticisms to his Studio with a cigarette dangling from his lips and dropping ash as he went.

However without Ruby and even with the company and assistance of Betty and Leon, life appears to be getting a little bleak for the aging widower. He appreciates the help of his daughter and son-in-law and in a Christmas letter to Joe in December 1962, acknowledges that: *Betty is a fine lass - she works like a trojan - both inside and out. Leon is fine too - he does all the heavy jobs here - apart from teaching German and Art at the school.* The letter is short and he admits: *I really don't know what to write about - things are so very quiet here . . . I'm just lazy from morn till night.*

Joe and family are now settled in Edgewatee Drive, Boston, Massachusetts and at some point after that Christmas letter, the decision is made for Betty to take her father to see her brother in America. James is obviously looking forward to this trip and reunion. He writes an even shorter letter on April 21st 1963, (incidentally the anniversary of Ruby's death although he doesn't mention this). Again he is apologetic about his lack of energy: *I don't know why it is, but I don't seem to be able to do anything but sleep and eat.* He also bemoans the long winter, a phenomena I recognise living just down the road from Millbeck Place! *I wonder what the winter has been like with you. Here it has been awful and even now there are patches of snow on the mountains.* (The winter of 1963 was a particularly bad one with heavy snowfalls and icy conditions lasting for many weeks and in London Sylvia Plath committed suicide in February, although admittedly factors other than the weather were involved.)

However James has things to look forward to . . . there are signs of Spring in the air and the garden - after hard work by Betty - is beginning to look good.

Again we can see how much he values Betty. Leon comes in as a bit of an also-ran but James recognises that *I would be in a pickle without them.* He refers to the imminent American trip with the words: *I am looking forward to seeing you all again in a very short time and rather ruefully and with fine irony observes I wish you were all over here, but perhaps you like Boston rather than Keswick.* It's signed: *Yours affectionately, Dad.*

The proposed trip to Boston took place later that year. I

thought that this must have been the last time that he saw the American family, but a condolence letter to Joe after his father's death indicates the contrary. It's a heartfelt and lovely letter from Nan and Bob Brodie who were lifelong friends of James and Ruby. Nan writes from her home address in Surrey on the 10th November 1964:

I feel very heartbroken over your Dad's death. He seemed so much better after your visit and we left him with Kathleen looking so cheery at the gate. I am grateful he was not ill for long, but wish he had been at home. It seems somehow like the last break with my youth. I remember both your Mother and your Dad before they were married and seem to have been thinking of those days all today.

I hope you got through all right as today is very heavy fog. Perhaps it is clear up north. I would have liked to say goodbye to Jimmie, but we seem so far away and things are so uncertain. I am so glad Jimmie saw Janet. He was so proud of her woodcut and of her.

Lovingly yours ,
Auntie Nan and Uncle Bob.

Nan's letter is written the day after James' death and his death certificate provides the details. He died in the Cottage Hospital in Keswick on the 9th November 1964 of hyperlactic pneumonia and cerebral thrombosis.

Leonard registers the death on the 11th November and is described as 'son-in-law in attendance'. Hopefully Betty was also by her fathers's side at this time.

The funeral, which took place on Thursday, 12th at Crosthwaite Church, was conducted by the Vicar, Canon F.H. Marshall. Joseph, Betty and Leonard are described as *chief mourners, alongside Mrs Jack Ellis, Workington (sister-in-law) Mr Wilfred Ellis, Lockerbie, (brother-in-law) and Ruby's two nieces, Mrs Harry Grice (this is Denise) and Mrs J. Iredale (Yvonne) and her husband.*

The Keswick Reminder obituary states that he was buried as he wished in the peace of Crosthwaite churchyard.

A simple slate headstone marks the last resting place of

James Durden R.O.I and his name is inscribed underneath that of Ruby with the words *Her devoted husband.*

The top curve of the stone carries the words 'IN LOVING MEMORY OF' and these form a semicircle above a circular motif of a stylised tree which was designed by Durden after Ruby's death. It stands at the end of the row of three matching Ellis gravestones.

In the following weeks two obituaries appeared in the local press. The one in the Keswick Reminder published on December 13th 1964 was contributed and Janet thinks that it was possibly written by Betty. It is a sensitive and perceptive tribute to Durden, covering his ability as an artist and showing a real understanding of the nature and personality of this quiet and gentle man. His achievements are acknowledged: *At the R.C.A. he polished his sensitive handling of paint, his rich feeling for for tone and colour. His works, equally professional in watercolour and oils, became a notable feature in the dominant London Art Exhibition. His large figures were notable year after year in the Royal Academy. His beautiful landscape paintings enriched for years the annual exhibitions of the Royal Society of Oil Painters where he was elected a Member. The Paris Salon honoured him with medal awards . . . He developed a gentle sensitivity to the delicate and constantly changing light and tone of the valleys and fells. Some of his most successful works are of Lakeland subjects bathed in sunlight . . James Durden's works reflected his sincerity, his very gentle and peaceful nature, a reflection of the true peace he found in the natural beauty of the Lakeland valleys and fells around him.....'*

This heartfelt and sympathetic obituary finishes with the words: *James Durden was a man of peace, with a quiet and friendly word for all who met him, a kind and gentle man. His passing will be a loss to the valley, but his works will continue to give peaceful visual pleasure around the world.*

The obituary in the Cumberland and Westmorland Herald on November 14th 1964 echoes the sentiments highlighted in the Keswick Reminder. The headline reads: *OLD ENGLISH GENTLEMAN* with a topic line of *An Artist of High Repute.*

The rather sparse biographical details are given and he is described as: *not only a brilliant artist, but one of the most charming personalities among the many who have found a home in the Keswick district.* This obituary also quotes the words of an (unacknowledged) critic: *His feminine types are dainty and very modern and he delights in elegance and sophistication and the beauty pertaining thereto. His chief trait, in common with other Manchester born artists, is his adherence to light, clean colour and other qualities foreign to Lancashire. He missed no opportunity of painting sunshine seen through windows with all its reflections and values and loved the flash of light on glass and polished wood.*

Rather in keeping with this quiet and unassuming character,

it would seem that after his death Durden the artist quietly and peacefully settled into rather gentle obscurity. He remained in affectionate esteem within his own Lakeland home and by his own family, but was largely forgotten by the wider cultural world.

The final Exhibition, in November 2021 through the winter into Spring 2022, also focused on Betty's own work and her sketch book was viewed with interest. More importantly this exhibition triggered the biographical research into James Durden and Janet's Archive brought much hitherto unseen material into the public arena. This, combined with other research, produced documents, sketches and especially photographs which revealed some of the life of the artist. It was a life going from the industrial streets of Manchester, through hard graft and difficult times during the war, to major achievements and recognition. Finally it was possible to meet the man as well as the artist. This was the gentle but driven family man who worked tirelessly at his chosen life's work and the artist who said: *If I see something I like, I paint it.*

On Easter Sunday afternoon, 2023 I walked down to Crosthwaite Church to lay a small bunch of Spring flowers at the foot of James Durden's gravestone. For once it was a glorious Easter weekend, with brilliant blue skies and a triumphant dazzling sun. Light and splendour touched everywhere in the churchyard and the daffodils, revelling in not having the usual fight with rain and winds, danced in truly Wordsworthian fashion. The church was blessed with a Resurrection Cross resplendent in sunshine-yellow flowers. James would have delighted in the light skylarking across the stained glass windows.

The Ellis / Durden headstones are in a mid-section of the churchyard beyond the North side of the Church. When I first started this research, they were quite difficult to find. But now my steps took me straight to James and Ruby without a second thought, and I laid my small bunch of daffodils at the foot of his stone with respect and affection. I stepped back with a sincere 'thank you' to him and his family for allowing me to get to know him and understand in some small measure how his life and work developed. I also felt I needed to ask his forgiveness for all the situations in his life that eluded me or confused his story. It is my dearest wish that I have done him justice and passed an understanding of both man and artist on to the wider world, however badly, but always in good faith.

As I left the church gates and strolled along Church Lane, a young lad passed me riding a bicycle. The bike was an old one, rather ramshackle and decrepit but still cheerfully functioning. The cyclist was equally cheerful. Clad in shorts and a tee-shirt, he looked vaguely familiar (the benefits of teaching in Keswick for so long!) He was very happy to greet me with a grin and a Cumbrian *al-reet* as he carried on up the lane. He looked about 17 and I wondered if he would ever cycle a long way in search of a dream!

ACKNOWLEDGMENTS

I would like to reiterate my huge thanks to the Durden-Hey family, especially Janet for her permission to use so much valuable archive material in her possession and for sharing her memories of her grandfather with me.

My grateful thanks to the following:

Jenny (Catherine Jennifer Hey) for lending me a copy of her delightful book *HIGH GARDEN* featured in Chapter 14, describing the adventures, botanical and otherwise, of her grandfather Joseph;

All the staff and volunteers at Keswick Museum (formerly Keswick Museum and Art Gallery) for their interest and practical help. My especial thanks go to curators Nicola Lawson and Decks Skinner, and to Pam Herbert.

Margaret Martindale, Hannah Williamson, the Curator of Fine Arts at Manchester Art Gallery, Alan Mathewson, John Temple, the late Charles Nugent, Peter Nelson and Alan Edward, Graham Paterson and the late Kath Paterson, Alex Milner, Curator of the Beacon Museum, Whitehaven, and volunteer assistants Pam and to Magda and John and Bobbie Crosbie of Birkett Wood Farm.

Finally another thank you to my husband Dave - More proof reading, checking text, discussing my approaches and providing an unfailing sounding board at all hours of the day (and night!). All this is so much appreciated.

Copyright: Ros Roberts
First edition 2024
ISBN 978-1-912181-73-5
Published by Bookcase, 19 Castle St., Carlisle, CA3 8SY
01228 544560 bookscumbria@aol.com
Printed by The Amadeus Press.